The Way We Were

The Way We Were

JOCELYN GREENING

Published in 1991 by
The Self Publishing Association Ltd
Lloyds Bank Chambers
Upton-upon-Severn, Worcs
A MEMBER OF

in conjunction with
JOCELYN GREENING

British Library Cataloguing in Publication Data

A catalogue record for this book is
available from the British Library

ISBN 1 85421 130 7

Designed and produced by The Self Publishing Association Ltd
Printed and bound in Great Britain by Billing & Sons Ltd., Worcester

In memory of my parents, my sister
and the way we were.

The author trusts that she has caused no offence to past and present friends and neighbours. In sending them her best wishes, she hopes that they will accept the "tongue-in-cheek" comments in this book as they are meant to be, being entirely her own memories, and maybe not as her contemporaries saw times past.

EXPLANATIONS

I heard the gate open, and went out to see who was there. Standing at the door were two youths, one with a very swollen eye. They told me they were looking for the doctor's and I directed them and went back into the house. "My word!" I said when I had shut the door. "What a sting that boy has had, it wants the blue bag on it."

My daughter, a student nurse, looked surprised. It suddenly dawned on me that this was probably because she didn't know what I was talking about.

I explained that the remedy in my youth, was to take a square of *Reckitt's Laundry-Blue,* tie it up in a piece of cloth, wet it and hold it on the sting.

My daughter said, as daughters are apt to do: "What a hoot!"

Well, think I, what other stylish pastimes and memories would be a "hoot" to the youngsters?

So I started to think, and here are the results – my thoughts and memories of the 1930s.

CHAPTER 1

AILMENTS AND FRAILMENTS

Once upon a time, we were led to believe by our mothers that we couldn't exist without woolly vests, liberty bodices, thick enveloping knickers, garters, gaiters, boiled eggs, cabbage, apple-dumplings, zinc ointment, syrup of figs, scarves, hats, cod-liver-oil and malt, brimstone and treacle, *Virol*, and camphorated oil – which they rubbed vigorously on our bony chests.

We were also taught to be frightened of horses, thunderstorms, rabid dogs, bulls, swans (who could "break a man's arm as liv' look at him") and ostriches (who could do likewise to his leg/legs).

Most of these things led to nothing healthier than resentment, particularly in the sicklier variety of child such as my sister and me. The school clinic once wrote to my mother, advising her to administer my sister with fried bread and bacon fat which would "improve" her health after an illness of rheumatic-fever and its consequences.

According to the school medical officer, Mr Wyndham-Parker, she should observe the instructions on the following letter:

TELEPHONE No. 1200 (7 LINES)

WYNDHAM PARKER, M.C., M.B., CH.B. (EDIN), D.P.H. (LOND.) COUNTY AND SCHOOL MEDICAL OFFICER.

WORCESTERSHIRE COUNTY COUNCIL.
EDUCATION COMMITTEE.

PUBLIC HEALTH DEPARTMENT,
COUNTY BUILDINGS,
WORCESTER.

19th February 1937.

Sir or Madam,

MEDICAL INSPECTION OF ELEMENTARY SCHOOL CHILDREN.

One of the Assistant School Medical Officers has examined Margaret Taylor (12) and, as the child is delicate, I advise that the following precautions should, where practicable, be taken, viz. :—

1. Always sleep with the bedroom window wide open and in a bed alone.

2. Be out-of-doors as much as possible in the day-time, and never sit in a room with the window shut.

3. Should be encouraged to eat as much as possible, and if not eating well should be given Cod Liver Oil. Bread fried in bacon liquor is particularly nourishing.

4. Should wear flannel or wool next the skin, and never sit in wet boots.

Yours faithfully,

WYNDHAM PARKER,

School Medical Officer.

Some children, my sister among them, after suffering a debilitating illness, were sent to Malvern Open Air School. The School, tucked away somewhere in the hills, was designed to toughen and strengthen weak children by a vigorous diet of good food and fresh air. My sister hated this place. Never again, she said, would she eat prunes and custard – this, after being made to sit on the stairs one day until she agreed to eat her morning prunes. Her retaliation was to catch scarlet fever from a boy named Michael Taylor-Moore, after which she was sent to a fever hospital in Worcester, an altogether happier place, she decided.

Since time first began, it seems, the weak and the strong have battled side by side. In my childhood, we were either strong as cart horses, or delicate; there was nothing in between. And the "strong" would sneer as cod-liver-oil and similarly health-inducing medicines were poured into us weakies.

My mother was always worried about something, and consulted the doctor if she so much as discovered that I was sleeping on my stomach. She probably imagined I would squash my "inards" in doing so. All mothers lived in constant fear that we would catch diphtheria, measles, scarlet fever, whooping cough, typhoid, smallpox, or worst of all - tuberculoses; perhaps I should have said "the mothers of small families"; those with a large brood generally taking a "what is to be will be" attitude.

Mothers of large families that contracted measles, used to put all their children in the same bed, resigned to the fact that sooner or later they would all catch it together. Measles was a dangerous illness then and when our entire school of forty children came down with it, two actually died as a result of complications. Children were invariably left with a bad chest or weak eyes – at least we thought so: maybe the measles had nothing to do with it. I guess we were not far away from the image of pale, loitering Victorian infants and our mothers still had memories of sickly, ribboned and frilled children, propped up on feather pillows and smiling sadly at the camera for one last nauseating photo in this world. We were shown many such old photographs and told, sadly: "He was never right from the moment of birth, poor little so and so."

The book I adored all through childhood was *Little Women*. When I was reasonably fit and well, I was Jo March, with all her robust, tomboyish vigour. When suffering from one of my countless ailments, I was Beth, reclining on a cushioned sofa, preparing my beautiful thoughts for the next world.

The fear of tuberculosis was the prime terror. If one looked healthy, with nice red cheeks, there were mutterings of "too feverish" and "red cheeks a bad omen". If one looked pale and wan, it was the same. You couldn't win!

At one time my sister and I wore iodine lockets, tied with white tape and hung around our necks. My aunt, who was nanny to two children in Surrey, sent lockets to us, believing firmly in their qualities; they were supposed to keep away all germs and impurities and leave us as white as the driven snow. Goodness knows I was white enough already, well - more yellowish, as a result of my frequent ailments.

The school doctor came to visit twice a year. I was always on his list as being "delicate", an aftermath of the aforesaid measles. We used to be examined in the infants room, the rest of the school leaping up at the windows to have a good titter at our expense. The first doctor I remember was fat and wore spats. He rejoiced in the lovely name of Dr. Clover. When he retired, another pleasant little man took over - very gentle, who, seeing the spots and blotches of red upon my chest and back, smiled into my knee-caps (he was very small) and told my mother: "This child suffers with her nerves."

Well, this was extraordinary, for in those days people just didn't suffer *with* nerves. Nerves were things that you *got on*. Nerves were certainly not considered anything to do with bad health; we were just "delicate".

From there on, I was away to a fine start. Everything was blamed on my nerves: tiredness, boredom, bad temper, sulks, the weather, bags under the eyes, bad summers, fear of the dentist, the Nazi uprising and bilious attacks every morning around school-time. Whatever – "Poor little soul, she can't help it, it's her nerves" was always the order of the day.

Our own G.P., ever sharp and to the point, said to my mother:

"Send her to school, even if she's sick every inch of the way". I hated him!

We also had things called "strained hearts", "enlarged hearts", "growing pains", "St. Vitus' dance", and the particular favourite, "Out-growing our strength".

One thing we never seemed to suffer with were broken limbs and put-out joints. The most we could aspire to was a slight sprain, but that never even involved a visit to the doctor. When I was about seven, a boy who had recently returned to England from Canada and was staying with his Aunt Bertha round the lane from us, broke his leg. We were thrilled to bits: we'd never seen or heard of anything like it. When we were told we could visit him and take him our jigsaw puzzle to pass away the time (the jigsaw bit we resented), we couldn't wait. Dreadful disappointment! I expected to see his leg broken right off and lying on the table, but no, there it was, done up in a boring white case, resting on a chair and attached to his body as usual! This was probably my first major let-down in life. Of course, Georgie (said nephew) sat there looking listlessly pale, as was expected of him, but triumphant; his Aunt Bertha gliding around him in her long black dress excited at all the publicity her grubby cottage was receiving. I never forgave Georgie; what with his also going to Canada *and* getting our jig-saw, what could you expect?

Mothers were always on the look-out for ringworm, septic spots, nits and lice - in other people's children, that is. It was unthinkable, of course, that their own off-spring would have such things. The District Nurse came once a month to inspect our heads. Marching into the girls' porch in single file, Nurse Neal combed through our hair, with lovely gentle fingers. It was a great, soothing sensation, and we would be jolted back to reality as she murmured a gentle "That's all right, dear" down our ears. Secretly, I was disappointed when she didn't find anything: it was so thrilling to have my hair continually washed and combed to remove alien bodies. Inevitably, my sister and I did catch "things", as they were called; one occasion probably as a result of hanging our hats next to an infected hat on the porch pegs.

Contrary to what some parents believe, I do not think that children mind about half the things that are supposed to upset them. We lived in a poor community, in times when *real* poverty prevailed, and the last thing we wanted was to be different. We liked to look dirty, we liked to talk grammatically "bad". I used to brood silently over the fact that Mother didn't go to work on the land, as many others did then. I would have given anything to be able to boast that she was picking potatoes, or peas or fruit. At times I was bitterly ashamed that my grand-father had been a school head-master, especially as my teacher would pick me up on spelling mistakes in front of the class, saying: "You should know better with your background." The other children would stare curiously and giggle, while I blushed and cringed and hoped to die.

Children are inverted snobs, I suppose you could say!

CHAPTER 2

GRANDFATHER'S HOUSE

Auntie Bo was born on July 19th, 1878. Her real name was Florence Annie, or "Flo", but as often happens, one child in the family couldn't say Flo, so she became "Bo". She was my mother's eldest unmarried sister, seventeen years older in fact, so she was more like a grannie to my sister and me.

Auntie Bo was very small and very determined. She loved children, but did not openly show affection to them. She did not believe in smacking but had a sharp and effective tongue; she also had a positive phobia about dirty necks and would scrub and rub with carbolic soap until we shrieked for mercy.

Auntie Bo loved babies and thought they were all beautiful. She hated cats, was indifferent to dogs, despised men and loved robins – the robin was her symbol (as we would say today) and she used to draw one in the corner of all letters and notes that she sent.

Every year on her birthday – we never under any circumstances missed her birthday – my mother, sister and I would set off for a visit. We toiled through the hot apple orchard known as Dough Bank, up the steep hill, past Pearson's shop and the tethered goats, over the stile, up the Little Drover's Lane, under the oak trees, between the damp mossy sandstone rocks where Herb Robert and Hart's Tongue Fern grew, out into the lane by the green stagnant pond where the Waters' horse grazed, past the farm, and round the corner of the stone wall that surrounded Grandad's house.

We would arrive hot and sweaty, clutching at our home-made birthday cards, eager for the special tea of bread and butter, orange jelly, home-made egg-plum jam, David Grieg's delightful Dundee cake, and, if we were lucky, a sardine. The table would be laid with the second-best table-cloth, darned discreetly in the corner and the second-best tea set, obtained by saving tea coupons from *Blue Bird* tea packets.

When we handed over our cards, usually post-cards drawn over with thin, long-legged robins or square cross-eyed cats (we tried to please!), we would kiss Auntie Bo – who always smelt of carbolic and lavender. We didn't give presents, the present commercialism not having yet begun, though we may have taken a bunch of sweet peas from the garden and Mother perhaps a quarter of tea. Auntie Bo, exclaiming with delight at our offerings, would jam the flowers upright and stiffly in a vase, and stand the tea like a sentinel on the mantelpiece between the Boer War brass shell cases and the black marble clock.

Tea and conversation finished, we always hoped to start out for home at about seven o'clock, but, strangely, most years a thunder-storm intervened. Mother was terrified of tempests, as she called them (along with William Shakespeare), and would sit in the corner of the room with a table-cloth over her head so that she couldn't see the lightening. She would cajole Auntie Bo to cover up all the cutlery, scissors, mirrors and pictures, and forbid us children to get near the window or the doors; we were to speak in whispers and were not allowed to laugh, or indeed do *anything*, except crouch in the corner with her. Auntie Bo would laugh – she wasn't afraid. Grandad was though, and so were we children – a little. "Is it moving towards Worcester?" Mother would ask. "Or Kidderminster? If so, the storm's sure to come back!"

Only after the heaviest rain was it safe to venture forth, and we would arrive home to find Dad supping home-made wine to "keep the damp out", or helping to bale out the neighbours' flooded cottage where the drains had overflowed down the hill from the saturated fields.

Auntie Bo had lived for twenty-five years of her life as a companion to Great-Aunt Bolton in Birmingham. Great-Aunt B., reasonably well off, enjoyed many of the luxuries of the lower middle class, and Auntie Bo was allowed to share this life with its advantages and otherwise – theatre season tickets for the best shows; unlimited access to the fine art galleries and museums in central Birmingham; good food; plenty of warmth and no heavy work; until Great Aunt B., after resisting and defying her maker with gusto, eventually faded out a healthy and rigid ninety-three – incidentally, taking three weeks to fade.

When Great Aunt B. was gathered, Auntie Bo came home to keep house for her recently widowed father. She cared for him to perfection, gently moulding him into doing the things she "knew" were for his own good. She used to hurry around the garden, on hot days with his panama hat, on cold days with his jacket, scolding away as she went; or following behind him with the deck chair to find a suitable spot – not too hot, not too shady – for him to sit. By the time she'd finished fussing, he had usually given up and gone back to sit in his upright chair "For a bit of peace", as he said. I don't think he ever got his peace; even on winter nights she would devotedly set out down the long lane with candle-lantern or even candle-stick, to light Grandad's way back from a drink in the village pub!

Grandad was a gentle, humorous old man. He had retired prematurely from his job as school master, because of his "nerves". He must have been well into his seventies when I first remember him and I always think of him sitting in his chair by the fire, making spills for his pipe. His eyesight was very poor and he could not see to read. He used to shave with a cut-throat razor in the back kitchen, stropping the razor to the fascination of us kids, until Auntie Bo drove us away, fearful that we would worry him into cutting himself.

Auntie Bo was always breaking things – ornaments and such-like, and she was a great over-winder of clocks. There were about six clocks altogether that she had zealously "over-wound"; for a small person she was very heavy-handed. Grandad liked to tinker with these clocks, releasing the springs and trying to make them go. "Your Auntie Florrie'll soon break them again", he'd say, resignedly. We children would swing the pendulum madly, believing we were mending them too, until Auntie Bo pounced on us.

When Grandad wasn't making spills, mending clocks and shaving himself, he meandered around the garden he had created as a younger man. A real old-fashioned garden it was, with lavender, rosemary, stocks, London pride, pinks, moss roses, mignonette, sage and peppermint.

In the garden, in pride of place, stood a large holly tree. Every Christmas a man in a lorry came round to buy holly from us. He used to pay Auntie Bo thirty shillings (£1.50). Although the tree was her pride and joy, the money was very useful then. It could buy a small chicken (a particular luxury), a 1lb *Robertson's* pudding, a box of dates, a tin of peaches, a Dundee cake, and a little extra tobacco and a new handkerchief for Grandad's Christmas present.

Grandad's house, a small walled farmhouse with outside lavatory, wash-house, pig sty and well, was old, shabby and lovely. Life and death had passed contentedly within its walls since the 17th century. Sometime in its history it had been divided into two cottages, the other being a tied farm cottage for an estate worker at the court, and now occupied by the Daniels family.

Grandad came to live there in 1909. His nerves needed rest and quiet, and out of the four cottages available, he chose this, the most peaceful, surrounded as it was by orchards, meadows and earthen lanes. It was also the cheapest rent offered to him, at three shillings (15p) a week.

Through the old front door, which shook and rattled alarmingly, was the cool red-stoned hall. Centuries of strong country boots had worn the stones smooth, and the plaque over the sitting room door which said: "Peace Perfect Peace" seemed to describe the overall feeling of the old house.

It may be interesting to record that the agreement for the tenancy of this cottage, made on August 23rd, 1909 between Michael Edward Marcus, Lord Sandys and my grandfather Frederick Cottrell, reads partially, as follows . . .

The landlord to pay all rates and taxes. The tenant at his own expense to colour or whitewash in a proper manner, the whole of the inside of the said cottage and premises usually coloured and whitewashed as often as it shall be necessary, and also to keep the glass of the windows in good repair at all times during the Tenancy, and so deliver the same upon expiration of the Tenancy with the garden in good order and condition. No poultry to be allowed to run loose, no wood to be chopped inside the dwelling house, and no potatoes to be stored therein.

When we children were staying at Grandad's, Auntie Bo sometimes allowed us to help her in small ways. "A little help's worth a lot of pity," she'd say, as we threw the blankets out for airing. She was most fastidious. Beds had to be stripped and turned every day, even on Fridays, which most people said would "cause a death in the family." We had feather beds, of course, and they were heavenly to sleep in.

When we dusted the living room – always full of bric-a-brac – we had to move all ornaments and small things from the mahogany table to ensure that we cleaned them properly. These included a Bible box, a small mahogany box containing photos wrapped individually in tissue paper and tied with tape, two cut-glass vases, a blue glass Victorian vase with a simpering maiden peeping round a tree, a pile of Church magazines, hymn books, and the gramophone which our Auntie Nellie had brought from an exhibition in London; this latter was one of the first H.M.V. portables, a handsome small machine quite different to the old horned gramophones that people were used to.

The mantelpiece, which we were also allowed to dust (while Auntie Bo kept a careful eye because of the danger from the fire), contained various and plentiful things, such as the brass bullet case, the tea tin and Grandad's spills. In the centre stood the large clock presented to Grandad and Grandma upon their retirement from the school. Originally it had had a black marble eagle perched on the top, as did many similar clocks, but I understand that during the Great War, people broke the eagles off their clocks and threw them away: they were emblems of the "dreaded Germans". A clock with an eagle intact would be a collectors piece today.

In three corners of the room Grandad had put up little triangular shelves, also choc-a-bloc. One held a tin containing clean handkerchiefs (the tin had a little drawer concealed and a key which I loved to lock and unlock to my heart's content); another tin with candles, matches and Grandad's pipes and tobacco.

On another shelf were kept two paraffin lamps, one for week days with a single burner and one for Sundays with a double burner, that is to say one or two wicks. These Auntie Bo cleaned, and refilled daily, blowing and huffing and puffing down the lamp glasses and polishing them lovingly with a yellow duster. At night, when she lit the lamps she would say: "Lighten our darkness we beseech thee, oh Lord" or, "Let there be light." On this shelf was also kept Grandad's best hat which we were sometimes allowed to brush for him with a little stiff brush kept, specially for the purpose, beside the hat.

The last shelf contained a small tray with ink and pens. On "Royal" occasions, such as the King's birthday or the Jubilee, there would also be a picture of the King and Queen and a Union Jack; sometimes a large flag stating "God save the King"was draped over the whole lot! The button-back horse-hair chair was also usually festooned with pictures of Royalty. The baby Prince Edward and his mother Princess Marina were great favourites, as *she* was so beautiful and *he* had lovely curls.

In the last corner stood the much-loved and coveted harmonium, which we were allowed to play on - very infrequently as we might have "given Grandad a headache" Auntie Bo told us.

The room also contained one handsome, but uncomfortable horse-hair sofa, one cranky but comfortable old sofa, Grandad's high backed chair, and about six other dining chairs, and the table in the centre of the room.

The walls were covered in large pictures. The two favourites, *Cherry Ripe* and *Bubbles* by Sir John Millias, were the original posters advertising *Pears' Soap*.

You may think it all sounds very cluttered, but it was a large square room, formally the parlour of the farm house, and didn't give this impression at all. It was a lovely room, smelling of lavender, apples, paraffin and Grandad's pipe.

The black fire-grate, with the trivet for hanging on kettles and pans, was the only cooking facility until Auntie Bo in later years bought a little stove; this she kept in the back kitchen and took at least three quarters of an hour to boil a small kettle for tea. She was very proud of this smelly little stove, and kept marching up and down the long hall to see how the kettle was progressing. But we did miss the smoke-tasting tea, that had previously been made over the fire.

Electricity was never installed in the cottage and although it was 1964 when Auntie Bo died, she continued to blow the fire up with bellows, carry candles outside to the lavatory and generally rebel against modern amenities. In fact she carried a lighted lamp up the stairs every night to bed until she was eighty-six.

The large straight staircase leading to the upper floor had the strangest stairs, all pock-marked and crumbly-looking in white wood; they were never graced with any carpeting, so Auntie Bo used to scrub them once a week with soda and carbolic soap. They were dangerous stairs to a small child and I was quite eight years old before I would venture down without sitting out each step on my bottom!

Grandad slept in the back bedroom which had a sloping floor and led up from two wooden steps. Auntie Bo had the large front bedroom which could accommodate both a double and single bed, and had a dear little alcove for the wash stand. The cottage differed from most because, owing to the fact that it had once been a small farm, it had large corridors and landings and plenty of room for storage, whilst other villagers scrabbled and fought to find enough space for their large families.

My sister and I were born in a small cottage in the village. At this time the first council houses were being built in the district and into one of these we moved. Working classes would almost never buy their own house; it would have been financially impossible. So, most cottages were owned by the local lord, or the farmer, and rented out to people for approximately three to six shillings a week.

The only working class owners were the small-holders, whose property had maybe been passed down for some generations. I don't think the people concerned had any higher standard of living than us. They still accepted outside bucket lavatories and no drainage, cheerfully tossing their slops and washing water across their gardens.

We knew no different life. The council houses also had outside lavatories and no bathrooms, but were built in a much neater design, with a tiny recess for tool sheds. They did have drains, but where the water drained to, nobody knew – or cared! And the one water pump was shared by the six houses, which caused more than a few disputes as the "lower half" had to walk through the "upper half's" gardens to get to the pump. Sometimes a real rumpus got going, as the upper half refused access to the lower and the council would have to send someone in to arbitrate!

Unlike today, phrases such as "re-housing", "housing estates", "fair rents", etc., were unheard of. If you lived in the town, you lived in a street – or if you were "posh", an avenue; but in the country, you lived "up the road" or "down the road".

If you moved into a council house, you were either a slum dweller, or part of an overcrowded large family. I imagine, although I was too young to know much about it, one immediately lowered one's status by becoming a council house tenant.

My father was an embittered victim of the first world war, embittered in so much that his life revolved around his experiences in the trenches and his hard childhood. He could not stand wastage of any kind, and continually harked back to the lack of food around when he was a boy. He used to watch my mother throw out bread to the birds, in the freezing cold winters of those days, with a brooding resentment.

Severely wounded in both legs, and thwarted in his desire to become a shoe-maker or "snob" as they were called, Dad should never have had to work as hard as he did. Such was his martyrdom that he seemed to be driven to take on the hardest possible work, gardening and such like. He was a postman for many years in the village. Most men drank then, some moderately like my grandad, some with less restraint. We never knew how our father was going to arrive home after being out on the post-round, with only home-made wine to fortify him! I think home-made wines were the bane of most wives. They were potent and plentiful. Father would frequently fall down on the way home and have to be rescued by some passing farmer, who thought it highly amusing. We didn't find it so. Dad could never get on with our neighbours and fought a continual cold war with either side. It was therefore a happier situation when we moved again to a cottage half a mile further on, which was detached, surrounded by a large garden and practically neighbour-free.

We were still only half a mile from Grandad's cottage, which was our refuge and salvation.

CHAPTER 3

AUNTIES, UNCLES AND A FEW COUSINS

Apart from vandals, cigarette smokers, motor-bike addicts, drug pushers/pedlars and takers, and litter louts, I admire the younger generation of today, mainly for their honesty. They openly state exactly what they feel.

Instead of creeping in the back door on the dot of ten to avoid paternal wrath, as we used to do, they casually fling out a "See you", or "Shan't be late" in nonchalant tone. We parents tremulously take it on the chin.

When we were young, we were taught total dishonesty of feeling. We were expected to love without question the Royal Family, the Government, the Vicar, all in authority over us and of course, our relatives.

Our teacher would not tolerate anything less than cringing servility towards the upper classes. One boy in my class got himself caned for making a remark about Clement Attlee, then a rising socialist politician. He only referred to him as "Old Attlee", but that was enough to send Teacher into a terrible rage.

My mother was the youngest of a large family, and my father the middle of an even larger one, so we had an immense number of aunts and uncles. We probably had upwards of thirty cousins. Most of our cousins were old enough to be our parents. When one of their visits was imminent, we were given to understand that it was to be "a very exciting occasion", and I was usually sick with anticipation (my nerves, you will remember). When the aunts arrived, they were either clothed from head to toe in black, which was enough to scare even as tough a youth as Mickey Rooney, let alone such a timid child as me; or they were fashionably dressed ("fashion plates", we said) and plastered in face powder and lipstick, a strange thing to us kids, as our mother only used *Icilma* cream, rubbed well in, and occasionally *Tokalon* powder which she rubbed furtively on and hastily off!

Aunties always smelled of carbolic soap, mothballs, peppermint or *Eau-de-Cologne*. Uncles smelled of tobacco, mothballs and beer, and they wore bowler hats, stiff white collars and usually black suits, carrying raincoats over their arms.

Aunts and uncles visited us in the summer time, usually on bank holidays – Whitsun and August, and sometimes on birthdays, but always at the correct time – which they do not seem to do now!

On arrival, aunts (wearing their hats at *all times*) went straight into the house to sit down in the shade with the curtains drawn and to drink tea which they often poured into their saucers to cool.

Uncles were pounced upon by Dad and taken on a tour of the garden – whether they liked it or not – in order to admire the fabulous fruit and flowers and the majestic vegetables Dad grew, which uncles could *not* in their tiny town-type gardens. They were expected to gasp with admiration and awe at these wonders so boastfully displayed.

Afterwards uncles joined the aunts in the house. They removed their bowler hats and sat on the edges of chairs, clutching hats and smoking nervously. Aunts always said without fail to me: "When are you going to stop growing?" or to Mother: "When is she going to get a bit fatter?" casting fond looks on their own fat, large-busted, red-cheeked daughters.

We were expected to kiss our aunts and uncles on arrival and departure. The aunts' part wasn't too bad, (remember the *Eau-de-Cologne*?) but the uncles always smelt beery and that was not at all pleasant.

Some of our aunts and uncles were as much a trial to us as Maggie Tulliver's were to her! They regarded us peasants with open scorn and pity because we did not have electricity, smart carpets, three-piece suites, water lavatories, bathrooms, piano lessons or our windows cleaned regularly by a "man". Neither did we have milk in bottles from the Co-op, as they did, but delivered in a churn straight from the cow to the jug, by local farmer Mr Hyde. They disregarded the fact that we had large gardens with fresh vegetables and fruit – which they were always delighted to take by the armful back to town.

These were only some of our relatives. Of course, some were very interesting and many, much loved. Two of the popular ones were Uncle Harry and Auntie Laura. Harry was a jovial, witty man, a veteran of the Boer War. He had been a sergeant/farrier with the Worcestershire Yeomanry, and like my father had been wounded in the Great War. He wore a woolly sock on a shattered wrist and was famous for the fact that he had had nineteen operations to date (a vast amount in those days), mostly to remove shrapnel and bone splinters that had worked their way round various parts of his body. He used to tell us fantastic stories of his life; like how he was once given a Stradivarious violin by his uncle which was promptly put into the dustbin by Laura, who couldn't abide clutter in the house.

He also told us the tale of a cat that he had taught to box, having made it a pair of miniature boxing gloves. He vowed that people came from near and far to watch the performances.

Although we took most of his tales with a pinch of salt, one story he told we believed whole-heartedly – he had a photograph to prove it. This was the story about the time he was working as a vet's assistant in Banbury: Lord George Sanger, of circus fame, approached him and, admiring his handling of horses, offered him a job taking care of the circus horses. The photo showed Harry shoeing the largest horse in the world, an immense animal weighing about two tons and belonging to the Sangers.

Auntie Laura was a smart, good-looking lady, tightly corsetted and permanently waved. She had no time or patience for the countryside, from which she had gladly escaped upon getting married.

They always visited on Grandad's birthday, August 4th and we usually went out "en masse" to meet them down the long lane. The bus stop was a mile away from Grandad's house, and to see Auntie Laura tottering yards behind the rest in her court shoes and tight skirt was a painful experience for all!

She always seemed to be clutching a lace-trimmed handkerchief to her nose to keep out the terrible smells of the country. The most amusing thing was when she visited the outside lavatory: she was convinced that she would find a rat waiting to attack her on the seat. Someone had to stand outside with a stick to bash this mythical rodent and save her from a terrible fate. After years of moaning, shrieking and gasping with fear, Auntie Bo suggested that she use the willow pattern chamber-pot upstairs. This she agreed to, gratefully at first, though after a time she developed a rat complex about the upstairs area as well.

Auntie Laura always brought Auntie Bo a quarter of *Eastern-Tips* tea. Auntie Bo would purse her lips and accept politely, if dubiously, as the tea came from the Co-op: she deeply distrusted such things. She had to admit it made a good cup of tea – thanks to the pure well water, which caused Laura to shudder at the thought of frogs and snails and such-like that would *never* get into town water.

We country dwellers couldn't understand her behaviour. We accepted rats and mice and frogs and snails as part and parcel of our lives. But Auntie Bo, sardonic, yet ever loyal, emphasised what a *wonderful* wife Laura had been to Harry, and couldn't help these strange performances.

Auntie Laura lived to a great age, and was smart and fashionable to the end. When she was well over eighty, she fell and broke a leg. We visited her in hospital and found her agitatedly dishing out instructions to her daughter Doris to look out her best bed-jacket and most glamorous nightdress; bemoaning the fact that her hair had not been set for two weeks; and goodness knew what a fright she looked!

Cousin Doris (my god-mother) was an exciting person to us; she was at least twenty-five years older than me. Although having a humdrum job in a draper's shop, she seemed to live a gay existence, going to dances and entertainments all the time, having hosts of friends and being engaged to a dance-band leader.

Her brother Cecil, though witty like his father, led a quieter life. He nicknamed me "Lightening" on account of the fact that I was always rushing about – usually trying to find some place to hide as I was so shy of meeting these cousins (my nerves, you will again remember!).

Another aunt I was fond of was Annie, my mother's sister-in-law. She was renowned for being a wonderful cook, and made delightful fruit cake, full of juicy fruits and red cherries, and of a lovely rich dark colour – the sort of cake that children loved, but were seldom allowed to eat because "It will make you sick, it's too rich" (they said).

I was never afraid of Aunt Annie, as she made a big fuss of me. She was a stout lady, and would sit me on her ample lap and feed me gooey chocolate sweets: "Are you pleased to see Auntie?" she would purr. *I was.*

Aunt Annie's husband was Mother's brother, Fred. He was tall, thin and gentlemanly; he had been in the Royal Flying Corps in the First World War. Come to think of it, our family put in quite a good showing in the two wars, five uncles and one father in the first and one uncle (Roland) and numerous cousins in the second.

I have often pondered why we had no unusual names in the family. We had three Auntie Annies, two Auntie Nellies, two Uncle Freds and three Uncle Harrys. My grandmother (maternal) had the most attractive name: Julia.

Although they lived in the Worcester area I never actually met Cousin Doris (mark 2) who married a builder and had twin sons; Cousin Charlie who was also in the building trade; Cousins Billy and Harry who lived "up north"; or Cousin Tommy, who also lived "up north".

It was in the winter of 1930 during a snow storm that Cousin George turned up. Cousin George was another Northerner. He worked on the railway and played the cornet in a famous brass band. He continued to "turn up" at intervals throughout my childhood. We children welcomed him as a diversion. Our parents didn't.

Cousin George was a boozer and a boaster. He would make off to the nearest pub as soon as it opened, with Dad in tow. Mother didn't go much on this. Dad wasn't much keen on him either. I think he resented the fact that George appeared to know everything. "Come on, Uncle Ernie," Cousin George would say, "I'll show you how to do it."

"B . . . y braggart," Dad would grumble. "Thinks he knows it all!" Dad was so off Cousin George that when he got wind of an impending visit, he'd keep a sharp look-out for him. Upon seeing his approach, full tilt down the hill, with a large trilby resting on his jug ears – Dad would hurry us in, shut the doors and pretend that we were out. But that wouldn't deter Cousin George in the slightest. His head would appear at the window: "Hello, Uncle, hello, Auntie, hello, cousin," he would shout cheerfully and Dad would gloomily have to open the door to him.

Cousin George's final appearance, clad in army uniform, was during the war at our grandfather's funeral. As the coffin was lowered into the ground Cousin George stood stiffly to attention and saluted, watched by his astonished Aunts and Uncles.

We looked forward eagerly twice a year to the holidays of our very favourite Auntie Nellie. She was the nanny in Surrey, and greatly respected by her employers. My sister and I thought she was "just great". She was kind and generous, bringing us presents and regularly writing us letters and pretty post cards, and sending marvellous things at Christmas: a most popular person with all the family.

Looking back now and being more acquainted with young children, I suppose she had an arduous life caring for babies and the fractious children of wealthy people. There were advantages, of course: she travelled everywhere with them. We used to sit enthralled as she told us stories of holidays they had taken, sometimes abroad. She loved her children dearly, they were her whole world, but she always arrived home very tired, and we children were told not to worry her with questions. We were so eager to spend every minute of her holiday with her, we must have made ourselves a considerable nuisance; but if we were, well, she didn't show it, and was always patient and smiling, ready to go for walks with us to our favourite spots. It seems strange now that though she was supposed to come home for a restful holiday, I can never remember her once having a cup of tea in bed or a lie-in. Those things were just not done then.

And into the category of "aunts" must come our honorary aunt – Gladys, my mother's friend and sister's god-mother. Auntie Gladys was the infant teacher at a village school, a lively person. Although pretty-well middle aged, she was very "with it", as we would say today.

She played tennis, joined clubs and committees, dressed fashionably and smartly, and had many "gentlemen friends", but didn't marry until later in life. Every Sunday she used to walk up to Grandad's house to tea; she liked to discuss school matters with "the governor" as she called him. We always went to see Grandad and Auntie Bo on Sunday afternoons, so we saw a lot of Gladys. Sometimes a gentleman friend would collect her after tea and take her off for a spin on his motor-bike and side-car, or car.

Gladys tried hard to modernise Auntie Bo. Once, they had a week's holiday together in Bournemouth and before they went, Gladys insisted that Auntie Bo move the bun from the top of her head "à la Victoriana", to the back of her head in Twenties and Thirties' style. Auntie Bo didn't go much on this, but as she was looking eagerly forward to the holidays, she reluctantly agreed, though it has to be said, the minute they returned from Bournemouth up went the bun onto the top to remain there until her dying day!

Auntie Bo's hair was an endless source of fascination and industry to us children. When we occasionally slept in her bedroom – "emergencies" and so on – one of us shared her double feather bed, and the other had the spare bed. We both clamoured for the spare bed in the corner, because from there we had a better view of Auntie Bo washing at the wash stand, which was in the little alcove behind the door (I don't think we were *supposed* to watch these proceedings, so we pretended to keep our eyes respectfully closed). First thing in the morning, she would remove her voluptuous nightdress and put on her knickers and corsets, still wearing her vest which she changed every night at bed-time. The vest had short sleeves and was fastened at the neck with a ribboned bow. She soaped and soaped the flannel – this took quite a minute – then she went round and round her neck, face, ears, hands and arms; there wasn't much of her neck available so I suppose she made up for it by extra soaping on the parts that were visible. Finally came the rubbing and drying with the towel. She would rub her face until her poor little nose stood out like a red cherry. (Auntie Bo's actions on all matters consisted of round and round, and up and down, be it conducting her toilet, black-leading the grate, dusting, polishing or darning her stockings. Her darning was done so rigidly and vigorously that her stockings finished up with hard firm bumps all over the feet, and button holes so much over-sewn that the buttons would never do up again.)

After the washing and drying, she would take her false teeth from the basin in which they had been soaking overnight, pop them into her mouth and give us a *grim grin*. She would put on her petticoat, jumper or jumpers, skirt and stockings (three pairs in winter, two in summer) and buttoned shoes which she fastened with a button-hook. Then came the hair bit. She actually had very thin hair, but it was long, and she would comb it up and down, down and up, round and round, backwards and forwards and forwards and backwards. Then she twirled it into the bun on the top, jabbing great strong hair-pins into her scalp, while we children winced and gaped in fascination. During the day, due to the state of Auntie Bo's thin hair and the hair-pins being too large, they used to fall out, anywhere and everywhere, constantly. So, as she bemoaned the price of the hairpins, we would have to search all over for them. We were always relieved to pounce on these pins and return them to their grateful owner, who refused to consider trying out the new light weight pins, in spite of pressure from Mother and Gladys.

Auntie Bo was very odd about her corsets. She hated them, I suppose all women did as they must have been very hard and uncomfortable. On hot days it was nothing to see the sitting room door suddenly flung open wide and Auntie Bo's corsets come hurtling across the room after she had exasperatedly taken them off.

"There, take that!" she'd say.

"Florrie!" Grandad would say, "One of these days you'll do that when the Vicar or Lord Sandys are here."

"I don't care," said Auntie Bo, "It'll do them a power of good!"

CHAPTER 4

AND OTHERS

During the time that Auntie Nellie was on holiday at Grandad's, a friend of hers, a little lady named Florence, occasionally arranged to come from Stourbridge to spend the afternoon. Florence had been in service as parlour-maid in one of the houses where Auntie was formally a nannie. She was a smiling chattering little body, and a source of constant amusement to my sister and me. She had two sisters named Milly and Tilly whom she doted on and whose names she quoted in every possible sentence: "As Tilly said to Milly", or "As Milly said to Tilly", or "As I said to Milly and Tilly", it became quite hilarious. I remember the last time she came to tea, we two little girls were at the giggling stage, and during tea (Dundee cake, jelly, home-made jam, etc.) Florence, who never stopped talking long enough to draw breath, was well away with one of her usual Milly and Tilly sagas; it was just too much – I burst into loud giggles, followed by choking, followed by my sister likewise, followed by Auntie Bo joining in loudly and heartily. The trouble was that when Auntie Bo really laughed, she was quite unrestrainable and she would rock to and fro with tears pouring down her nose, which grew redder and redder. The aftermath was that the whole party shrieked and screamed with hilarity until we were all exhausted, while Florence, smiling obliviously, continued chattering on about her Milly and Tillys. The poor little soul!

As she said goodbye and set off to catch the bus she expressed delight at the lovely happy time she had had, little realising the cause of it all. We felt very guilty afterwards. Auntie Nellie was terribly ashamed at this treatment of her friend, but the mere mention of Milly and Tilly set us all rocking about uncontrollably for weeks to come.

Another strange character who came to visit for a few days while Auntie Nellie was on holiday, was a Miss Mattie. She too had been a nannie in very exalted households; she was in Egypt for years as nurse to King Farouk's cousin. She hated Farouk and declared that her own little charge should have been the rightful King. She used to tell us fascinating Arabian Knights-style tales of this period. Apparently, women in Cairo were not allowed out without male escorts, so when Miss Mattie insisted on going to market, much to her annoyance she had to be escorted by two large Egyptian solders from the Royal household guard, carrying drawn sabres and walking on either side of her. That at least was her story; we were always dubious about her as she appeared so much larger than life. She had bright orange hair, obviously a wig, and wore very tight steel corsets which creaked and groaned as she walked and caused her bottom to jut right out like Nellie Wallace's, the old music hall star.

Another amusing thing about her was the horse manure. Quite a few horses passed down the lane daily and each time, Nannie Mattie would rush out with shovel, sack and high hopes. She must have been successful, for by the end of her stay, she had accumulated a large sackful of dung to take back on the train to Manchester for her roses. How she transported it to and fro, I can't imagine, it must have been quite an operation. Auntie Bo didn't like her at all (I imagine neither did her fellow train passengers), but she was a terrific character.

Other visitors who popped in to see Auntie Bo included Mrs Allen, a gossip, who always wore a bit of moth-eaten fur around her neck in winter and summer. Grandad, who didn't care for her at all, said it was to hide the flea bites on her neck – he was convinced she never washed. Whenever he saw her coming, he reached for his cap and was quickly off down the road among the apple trees.

Auntie struck up another slight friendship with a middle-aged woman also named Florrie (we were snowed under with Florries, Flossies and Flos in those days; all Florences in England apparently deriving from Florence Nightingale who was christened after the town of her birth). When Florrie came to tea, it was always very formal – "Another piece of bread and butter, Florrie?" "No, thank you, Florrie" or "Try some Dundee cake, Florrie" "Thank you, Florrie." "Pass your cup, Florrie." "No more tea for me, Florrie, thank you." It was almost as bad as the Milly and Tilly saga.

This Florrie, though dull, was a very respectable person. One thing which annoyed Auntie Bo, Florrie had a dog named Nell (which incidentally *was* a dog and not a bitch, although we weren't supposed to know about such things then) and Nell would sit on Florrie's lap during tea. It was a fairly large brown dog, and quite quiet and boring, really. It never appeared to move, or bark or snarl or do anything that one expects a dog to do – maybe that was just as well as it used to place itself perilously near the Dundee cake. All the time during tea, Florrie would stroke the dog's head, up and down, up and down. We could sense that Auntie Bo was becoming agitated; she thought it was terrible to have a dog in close proximity to the food and didn't much care for animals anyway; she was simply too polite to complain to her friend. As soon as Florrie and Nell had departed around the corner with much waving and goodbye-ing, Auntie would rush in and sweep and brush and rub carbolic soap all over the place, even airing the cushions outside "to get rid of the dog germs".

One hot summer, we had a bevy of ultra-respected relatives

arriving from Birmingham, all crammed into a Ford car. There was Great-Aunt Annie, Great-Uncle Joe, Third-Cousin Emily, her son Archie driving the car and his wife Marjorie in the dickie seat.

Great-Aunt Annie was Grandma's sister and therefore Grandad's sister-in-law. Great-Uncle Joe was her husband. He had a large stout stomach and a gold watch chain stretching across it. Great-Aunt Annie was terrifically regal. Auntie Bo fussed and fidgeted for days getting the house spick and span and cramming Grandad into his stiff collar and best summer suit. It was a gloriously warm sunny day, and we had our photograph taken standing in a group by the wall, surrounded by the bearded irises. A pompous lot we looked too! Great-Aunt Annie and Uncle Joe were wealthy people and I think Mother rather hoped they would drop us kids a fiver. Great-Aunt Annie did give us sixpence and told us to be good children, and Auntie Bo and Mother each got a necklace of wooden beads, which went into their chests of drawers never to be seen again! So much for our wealthier relations.

We also had a visit from Canon Holding of Upton Snodsbury. He had been Grandad's friend when he was teaching and was very fond of Mother when she was a young child. He wore a long bushy beard and a panama hat. As he was driven away with much banging and shunting from the car, I remember the image of a small dignified figure clutching a gold-topped cane – sitting quietly in the dickie seat!

I must mention at this point Mr Nicholls. Though Mr Nicholls should come under the heading "Tradespeople", I think it only fair to his memory to put him on a higher pedestal. County people had much faith in, and affection for the tradespeople. We relied on them so much. The butcher who came out from the town stayed for tea; the milkman was given a hot drink in the winter; and the postman supped tea or home-made wine and in return brought us stamps, writing paper, ink, or anything else that we needed. Any of these would willingly give us a lift to the village, or deposit heavy suit-cases or boxes at a given spot. The baker delivered notes or Christmas and birthday cards by hand. Everything was splendidly self-sufficient!

Mr Nicholls didn't come into any of these categories. He was the agent for the coal merchant in Worcester and came once a month to take the coal order and collect the money for the previous month's coal. He also received and noted complaints, i.e. the quality of the coal and the exorbitant price – one shilling and sixpence per cwt (7½p) and conduct of the delivery men. In order to do these duties, he came out from Worcester by bus, had dinner at a customer's in the village and walked the mile to Grandad's house for tea.

Mr Nicholls was a person to respect. He was a large, florid Scotsman who wore tweed plus-fours, thick woolly socks with tassels, and smoked the most expensive brand of cigarettes. He talked and laughed loudly, stamping his brogue shoe until the floor shook and the tassels on his socks flew up and down. He used to stay the whole afternoon and when he departed he would leave two cigarettes for Grandad, which Grandad gave to Auntie Nellie who occasionally smoked, but very self-consciously and only on holidays.

Mr Nicholls referred to Grandad as "Sir" and Grandad referred to Mr Nicholls as "Sir". You could tell how exalted he was: at every Christmas he sent him an expensive religious card. We called him "Auntie Bo's sweetheart" and thought, in our ignorance, that one day she would marry him. I was terrified, but fascinated by him: he seemed so large and noisy. Auntie Bo used to complain to him about the dust and "bats" (pieces of slatey coal) in the coal, too much ash, and anything else she could think of, and Mr Nicholls would sympathetically write it all down in a little book. It was all done very quietly and politely on both sides.

It might be of interest to record a typical grocery order that Auntie Bo would send to the village shop – she certainly had a unique style of ordering!

As follows:-

½ lb best butter

2 lb sugar

4 oranges, my throat gets so dry in this weather

Packet Aspro, it might be a cold coming, it's the damp, I shall be glad when I get that patch on the bedroom wall done.

2 boxes of matches

1 lb sultanas

I hope your mother is keeping well, Mrs Smith?

6 candles, it doesn't do to run out

Have you any nice sausages?

A reel of white cotton

I wish you all a Happy Easter at the shop, and hope your leg has healed, my dear?

This is a copy of a grocery order dated 1935:*

	s	d		d
½ lb tea	*1*	*6 (7½p)*	*½ lb candles*	*7 (3p)*
2 lb sugar	*1*	*8 (8½p)*	*Boot polish*	*4 (1½)*
½ lb butter	*1*	*8 (8½p)*	*Powdered bath brick*	*2 (1p)*
½ lb cheese		*10(4p)*	*1 oz tobacco*	*10½ (4½p)*
½ lb bacon	*1*	*3 (6p)*	*Black lead*	*2 (1p)*
1 packet soap		*11 (4½p)*	*½lb Pearl Barley*	*3 (1½p)*

This was for two people for two weeks. No tinned stuff, you'll notice.

*All decimal prices approximate to old money.

CHAPTER 5

SCHOOL

I hated school. I hated the teacher, the class rooms, the smell of stale bread and jam, the smelly cloakrooms, the smelly lavatories and, most of all, I hated the smelly children.

I liked the ostrich egg on the shelf, the rocking horse in the infants' room, the piano, the holidays and the walk home.

I might have enjoyed some of the lessons, like history or literature, but we always had to study things like the Repeal of the Corn Laws, the Dissolution of the Monasteries, the Industrial Revolution etc. This was a right bore, we didn't want that! We wanted to hear about Henry VIII and what went on with his six wives. Geography just seemed to be about rainfalls, ice caps, Tibet and Borneo, and Teacher was nutty about yaks, of all things. We wanted to learn about America, especially Hollywood and its stars, but that wasn't on with Teacher!

I was always interested in books and poetry, but, it has to be said, most of my learning was at home; at the age of twelve, I was reading *Gone with the Wind,* while at school we were still being fed on fairy stories! Of course, you didn't dare admit at school that you enjoyed any learning, or you would have been jeered at or bashed by other kids.

Admittedly, we had a pretty good grounding in education in

village schools. We knew a little about a lot of things, which in my opinion is better than knowing a lot about one thing to the exclusion of all else. We were taught how to write properly, punctuation, spelling (very important), how to correctly word a letter, whether business or personal, and all this before we were twelve. The children of today miss out on much of this, I feel. For all their 'O' and 'A' levels they often haven't got a clue how to write a letter properly. Those old teachers were miniature encyclopaedias of general knowledge.

There were about forty pupils in our school. We were divided into an infants' group and a seniors up to the age of fourteen group (fourteen being the school-leaving age). There were two teachers, and two large rooms heated by weakly-smoking coal fires. The infants would straightaway be thrown in at the deep end and, within three days of starting school, would be reading the "cat sat on the mat" stuff . Many of the children were only three to four years of age. It was a status symbol to start at three. As our family was in the process of moving to our last cottage, I was a protesting five and a half!

It was cold and dull in the infants' room. In the corner stood the wooden rocking horse and a large doll's house, which we were never allowed to play with. What its purpose was, I can't think! But we little girls drooled longingly over it.

My first infant teacher was a very popular lady. She used to arrive at school on a motorbike, complete with leather coat, helmet and goggles and would be followed enviously through the playground by a string of small boys. She was strict but fair, and we did our best to please her. When she left, she was replaced by an older lady, whose sense of humour was somewhat questionable. One day this lady tottered into the classroom and said: "Now children, I want you to tell me if you notice anything different in my appearance." We remained very quiet. She started to get irritable. "Now, now, children, come along," she said.

One boy rose slowly to his feet saying: "Please, Miss, you've got some new false teeth," and blushingly sat down.

"Quite right, quite right," said Teacher happily, and took them out for us to admire. Another time she told us what she thought was a joke. Dead silence, not a titter. "Come on, laugh, children, all laugh, all laugh, or I will give you the ruler!" That did it, we screamed and rolled about in mirth until we were nearly hysterical. "All right, that's enough," said Teacher. "Now be quiet, children, be quiet, be quiet, I tell you or I shall punish you." Dead silence. It seems amusing thinking back on it now.

Moving up to the senior room was a time of fearful anticipation. You started off by moving from the infant line up in the porch, to the back line of the seniors, being elbowed and shoved like mad by the older ones, unless you had an elder brother who would come to your rescue and pummel and threaten your tormentors.

The senior room was larger and even colder. Round the walls were pictures of: The Boyhood of Raleigh and other portraits such as Nurse Edith Cavell, General Wolfe, King George and Queen Mary in Coronation Regalia; round the bottom of the walls were smaller pictures of poets and authors. We soon became familiar with the faces of Dickens, Byron, Browning, Keats and Barrie, though we knew little about their work. I always felt sorry for James Barrie, he looked so pale and sad. I couldn't connect him at all with Peter Pan, and spent many hours gazing at his poor countenance to the detriment of my work.

During my later period at school, the business of hygiene came to the forefront. We were given many pamphlets and talks on cleanliness – how important it was to wash our hands after going to the lavatory, and all that (never "toilet" or "loo", you'll note). In the school porch where we hung our coats and hats and played in wet weather, a mirror was hung behind the door; it was shaped like a lifebelt, with two hands clasped at the top to impress upon us how important it was to life and limb to be clean. A bit ironic, you'll think, when all we had to wash in was a small enamel bowl which was refilled with cold clean water once a day, and thought to be sufficient for the whole school. The bowl could accommodate about six pairs of grubby hands at a push, with much scrabbling and pushing to get to the carbolic soap. We never dared to replenish the water ourselves as the pump was outside on Teacher's territory and therefore out of bounds. I tried never to wash my hands at school, but this was difficult, especially after moulding plasticine or a painting lesson. One boy named Billy, who was not bright and thought to be uneducable by teacher, was in charge of the ablutions. He also sharpened pencils, filled up the inkwells, made up the fire and other menial tasks.

The lavatories were unspeakable! The girls had four buckets which were emptied once a week by the man who did Teacher's garden. The lavatories were at the back of the school and were of the usual country style with wooden seats. Our playground surrounded them, so we didn't play in this part much – the smell was atrocious. I tried never to use them either, but it was often difficult and painful to get through a whole day at school! When I later had a bicycle, I could get home for dinner, and my life was made a great deal easier. The boys' lavatories were adjacent to Teacher's. Sometimes a boy would emerge sniggering and pretend that he had seen Teacher pulling her knickers down. This improbable event didn't fool us for a minute!

Of course, in those days there were no school dinners. Most children took bread and homemade jam or dripping and we ate at our desks. School milk came into being at this time: a half-penny a bottle, or two and a half pennies a week. Parents moaned about the cost as many of them couldn't afford it, and eventually it was made free to all. I hated this milk and refused to drink it – it was pasteurised and not a bit like the lovely creamy milk delivered by churn straight from the farm to our home.

We also saw the advent of a new thing called Physical Training, or P.T., and the importance of this exercise was continually stressed – a bit of a laugh really when you think that some children had to walk six miles to school and back. On fine days we would be sent outside to gamble miserably, pretending we knew what it was all about, with our frocks tucked into navy blue knickers. With pleas of having colds, we managed to avoid tucking our frocks up; the jeering of the boys was too much to bear. The boys could leap around in their usual knee-length trousers, woolly jumpers and hob-nailed boots with tabs at the back, sparks flying. Teacher would don three cardigans, great-coat, scarf, gloves, woolly hat, and felt hat, and stand sheltering in the doorway, watching us doing our so-called exercises. On cold days, she actually stood inside the school watching us from the window, still wearing three cardigans, greatcoat and the rest! She was what we called then "a fearful starveling". I don't think she understood the benefit of P.T. any more than we did.

One day a lady came to school to look at our feet and legs and made us stand in a line. When she got to me she told me to hold my knees in; I did, but they shot out again, so she passed me by with a scornful glance. I thought I had committed some dreadful sin. We didn't understand what that was all about.

The highlight, and the worst fear of Teacher's year, was a visit from the school's inspector, Mr Cuttle. Thanks to the perseverance of Teacher, though her poor face always turned from a ghostly white to a sickly pea-green at the dreaded inspector's imminent arrival, our school always passed with flying colours. Sometimes we were allowed a half day's holiday to celebrate our victory.

A particularly exciting episode when war started, was the arrival of the evacuees from London. One boy came from Croydon and another, we were excited to learn, actually lived opposite the Houses of Parliament. One girl who came from London, had a terrible rash over her face and hands; her arms were bandaged and she always sat alone. The mothers chuntered like mad about this, fearing she had the plague or similar, I suppose, and warning their children not to go near her. It turned out that she suffered badly with eczema. Our mothers were not consoled, and remained convinced that we would catch it.

We locals treated the evacuees with scorn – scorn at their ignorance of the countryside, which was a pretty mean attitude when you consider that they had been torn away from their families and homes through no fault of their own. We also scorned the hop pickers' children. They came on an annual visit from the Black Country and stayed for about six weeks during September and October. The hop pickers' children were considered very lowly, and sat at the bottom of the room, separated from us and as far away from Teacher as possible. We used to really envy them for this, and would gang up against them in the playground; the boys fought them at every opportunity. But they usually emerged the worse for wear: the hop-pickers' kids were tough and had been brought up in a "rough" area.

CHAPTER 6

MORE SCHOOL

Although I hated the thought, sound and smell of school, there were a few aspects which were fun. When we first marched into school in the morning, there were always prayers and a hymn. We never had the usual hymn, ancient and modern, but instead little gems of songs which I have never heard since I left school – with the exception of 'Jesus bids us shine.' One favourite went like this:

If I were a beautiful twinkling star
I'd shine on the darkest night
I'd seek where the wandering pathways are
And shine there with all my might
Though sun or moon I may not be
To – oo make the whole world bright,
I'd find some little cheerless spot
And shine with all my might.

Another was:

Standing in the market place
Jesus watched the children play
He was glad to see them there
And he shared their happiness.
Praise to Jesus while we play
Praise him, praise him all the day.

and one favourite of mine:

A little lamb went straying
Among the hills one day
Leaving his faithful shepherd
Because he longed to play.
And while the sun shone brightly
He knew no thought of fear
For flowers around were blooming
And balmy was the air.
But night came over quickly
The hollow breezes blew
The sun soon ceased its shining
All dark and dismal grew.
The little lamb felt frightened
As well indeed he might
So far from home and Shepherd
And on so dark a night.

But soon the faithful shepherd
He missed the little thing
And onward went to find it
Safe home again to bring

He sought on hill, in valley,
And called it by its name
He sought nor ceased his seeking
Until he found his lamb.

Then to his gentle bosom
The little lamb he pressed
And as he bore it homeward
He fondly it caressed.
The little lamb was happy
So safe and free from harm
And happy too the shepherd
Because he'd found his lamb.

We bawled and yelled our lungs out with these little hymns. I think we all liked them. "Then to his gentle bo – o – som," we'd blurt. Bosom and breast were thought to be suggestive words and while Teacher was banging away on the piano keys, a deep flush would descend from her cheeks to her neck, while the big boys nudged and pushed and pointed at the girls.

We also had singing in the afternoon: lovely old folk songs such as 'Lincolnshire Poacher', 'John Peel', 'Randle, my son', 'Gossip Joan'.

"Jackie boy, Master, sing ye well, very well, hey down, hoe down, derry derry down," we'd shriek with delight. It was the only time at school we could really "have a go". Yes, we enjoyed that alright.

Poetry was another lesson regarded as important. Thanks to Teacher again, I can still quote a number of poems by heart.

Every term we each had to pick out and learn a poem to say aloud to the class. My favourite was Rupert Brooke's 'The Soldier', and I was well away with the learning of it one term. Upon returning after one of my frequent spells away from school, however, I found one of the boys had pinched my poem and I had to start all over again – left with only the unpopular ones to choose from, of course!

This boy, William, was a bad reader and very nervous; he had a speech impediment which didn't help matters and when he got up to say his (my) poem at the end of term, did I gloat! It went like this:

If I thoud die
Think only thith of me
Thattherthsomecornerofaforeighfieldthattithforever
Englanth . . .

At this point Teacher rapped on the desk and shouted: "Slower, slower, with expression." So off he started again:

If I thoud die
Think only thith of me
That there is thum corner of a foreign field that is
Forever Englanththerethallheinthisrichearch . . .

"Stop, stop," Teacher shouted enraged. Pool William, blushing and stuttering, started again:

If I thoud die
Think only thith of me
That there is thum
cornerofaforeighfieldthatithforeverEnglanth . . .

And so on and so on. Teacher wouldn't stand for that sort of treatment of English Literature.

But dang me, if this wretched boy William didn't do the same thing the next term; while I was away quietly being sick or something, he swiped William Blake's 'The Lamb' that I had set my heart on. It was very frustrating. We must have had an affinity or something, I suppose, picking the same poems, but I hated him of course.

While the boys had woodwork, we girls were given knitting and sewing lessons once a week. I was a good knitter and made myself a jumper when I was only eleven years old. The wool cost three pence (1p approx.) an ounce, three ply, so altogether the jumper cost two shillings (10p). It had to have long sleeves, as Mother wouldn't allow me to wear short sleeves in the winter for fear of catching cold; also, jumpers were strictly winter wear, not like today when sweaters are worn all times and any old time.

I was a rotten sewer. I was so tense and kept sticking the needle in my fingers. By the time I'd finished sewing a calico hem (hard material for petticoats) it was soaking wet with sweat, and dotted all over with red spots – the blood I had shed in the needlework cause! Teacher gave me some very funny looks when I took it up for inspection!

One girl named Vera knitted so tightly that she could not move the knitting along the needle; her hands were sweaty, like mine. She got into a terrible state when Teacher told her to undo it, as she couldn't even move one stitch off the pin; at each tearful attempt, the knitting squeaked and got wetter and wetter.

Another girl, Gladys, was exactly the opposite; if the knitting needle didn't have a knob on the end, she was such a loose knitter that as she finished the line, the beginning of the row was falling off the other end. She was good at making dish cloths, though; I often wonder if she knits her husband sweaters and if so, what they're like.

What a lot of Veras and Gladyses there were in those days! We also had a plentiful supply of Nellies, Dorothys, Roses, Marjories, not to mention Beatties. My name, however, was completely out! I was livid with my mother for giving me such a strange name, I would have swapped it for Nellie any day; it wasn't until I was grown up that I was pleased with it. In the boys, there were mostly Freds, Bills, Charles, Jacks, with a sprinkling of Stanleys and Ronnies.

Another thing we enjoyed at school was a very occasional nature walk. We used to go up the lane, past the Parish Hall, and down the road, passing proud parents who smiled and nodded at cottage gates. The boys had to sweep off their hats and wish the parents a polite "Good Morning" or "Good Afternoon" and the girls give a little curtsey. If we came across a pedestrian, we had to be extra polite and walk on the edge of the path, the boys standing with cap in hand until he had passed. Teacher was there at the ready with a thump in the back if we didn't come up to her expectations. She would walk at the back wrapped up to the chin in coats and woollies. Unfortunately, Teacher was no nature lover, being more concerned with our manners on these walks. She occasionally pointed out a tree to us or a blade of grass, but that was about it. The village pond was exciting as it had bulrushes growing, but these were too far out for us to get at. We never learned anything about bird life or flowers, I doubt if Teacher knew one species of bird from another and we were certainly never allowed near farm animals. I suppose their breeding habits would have been too difficult and embarrassing to explain. We knew a lot about yaks but nothing about our nearer neighbours, the cows and sheep.

We had "times" at school: times for chest-nutting, times for skipping, times for hopscotch, times for ball games, times for scrumping fruit and eating green gooseberries or goosegogs (a senseless pursuit, I never could understand it, but was too frightened not to join in); also, times for wearing different clothes. It was a terrific status symbol to be the first girl in a summer dress. It was never me though, as Mother firmly believed: "Ne'er cast a clout till May be out!" The first summer dress usually emerged about April, after the Easter Holidays. A shivering girl trying to look warm would stand in the biting wind with an admiring gang around her. Very soon many others would appear in their cottons. We "woollies" were ignored, and played miserably together, until the day we were allowed to wear our summer gear. Then all would be well and we would be accepted again. What snobbery it all was!

The same thing applied to hats and gloves when winter came. One year I had a terrific boost to my morale (and Heaven knows, I needed it). My Auntie Nellie sent me a matching hat and coat, a cast-off from one of her charges. It was a very smart outfit and hardly worn, a sort of red tweed. That put me higher up the social ladder than anyone else at school. To have a coat and hat to match was very classy. Then one day another girl, Gladys of the loose knitting fame, turned up in one, not such good quality as mine but never mind, we became "swarming" friends (another thing we used to say) and would stroll arm in arm about the playground with our noses in the air. Envious looks were cast in our direction but we ignored them. We were on a different plane. "Greater love hath no school girl than this, that she lay down her life for a matching coat and hat." Then came the matching dress and knickers era and, as we poked our hankies up the knicker leg, we would nonchalantly lift up the corner of our dresses, making quite sure the others saw how fashionable we were.

An ambition all girls had, was to wear a gym tunic, similar to the ones we saw in *Girls Own*, worn by the jolly hockey stick brigade who had midnight feasts in the dorm and crushes on Horace Rumbold or D'Arcy minor. Some of us achieved this ambition – the fat girls could fill out their tunics and look very smart; but I was so thin the tunic would hang on the bony edge of my shoulders and threaten to slip down at any minute. Besides that, Mother insisted I wear a cardigan over the top for extra warmth and somehow this spoiled the suave, debonair effect that I hoped to achieve.

We all envied Vera Peters, who was a fine strapping girl with a long blond plait and wonderful big legs. She did cartwheels in the school porch on wet days, to entertain us. She had doting parents who provided her with a variety of tailored gym-slips in different colours. Teacher continually pointed her out to us as a perfect example of how a well-dressed school girl should look; which was a bit unfair on the rest of us, when you think of the continual battle we fought in an effort to extract fashionable gear from our hard-up parents.

Another "time" we had was boasting time. We boasted about our families, our playthings, anything we possessed, places we'd been to and things we'd seen. Most children had never been out of the district, and when I timidly boasted that I had been on H.M.S. Victory at Portsmouth, and seen the actual place where Nelson had died, my best friend called me a liar, hit me and didn't speak to me all day. In the end I pretended that it really was a lie; then I was back in favour again. Strange that children would rather accept a lie than the truth.

It was the truth: thanks to my mother's frugality and perseverance, we had two happy holidays at Portsmouth – a strange state of affairs for working class people and we dared not talk about it at school as no other child had been to the seaside and we would have been severely ostracized.

One day during the boasting period, we were all going at it, trying to better the others, when one girl suddenly said loud and clear: "My Grannie Hammond's got a china egg." There was a deadly hush as we all stared at her in awe. We didn't know what a china egg was and I doubt if she did either! But it did sound exciting. She commanded much respect after that. I still don't know what she meant – don't suppose it was one of the Russian Easter eggs? No, never, knowing Grannie Hammond.

Teacher went mad one day and took us to Worcester to visit the Cathedral and art gallery. We enjoyed that, especially King John's tomb which I adore to this day. She told us about the thief who was flayed alive and his skin hung behind the cathedral door. We loved that. We gazed at the fragments of clothing and bones found in King John's tomb. We loved that, too.

The art gallery proved yet another embarrassment for Teacher. Pictures of nude females! One featured a large and bare-bosomed warrior – probably Brittania, her nostrils aflame with passion, and clutching a dangerous looking sword near her vital statistics. The boys enjoyed that, giggling and laughing and pointing until scarlet-faced Teacher hustled them on to the next picture.

CHAPTER 7

PATRIOTISM

We were a patriotic lot in the 1930s. On Empire Day, 29th May, we took our oak apples to school, set them in jam jars on the window sill and drew pictures of our national flags. We were also reminded by Teacher to wear a daisy, after all, weren't we all part of the Great British Empire? The scruffiest, dirtiest, most flea-ridden child in our school, was made to feel as important as the President of the United States of America that day.

Occasionally I would come under attack for not appreciating the fact that in order to get to school, I had to cross the River Severn which, Teacher declared, was the longest river in the British Isles. She would fix on me with a baleful eye, until she succeeded in making me feel an ungrateful little beast.

I only thought kindly of our river when it was in flood. There were terrible floods in those days and to be able to relate to my school mates that I had seen the bloated carcasses of pigs and sheep floating down stream, made me feel very important. Sometimes parts of landing-stages and boats that had broken their moorings sailed by, and once, a whole wooden bungalow went past!

During one of our more interesting history lessons on the Civil War period, Teacher asked around the class which side we would have supported, had we been alive at the time. All the girls favoured handsome King Charles, but the boys mostly plumped for Oliver Cromwell which caused Teacher to tut tut and purse her lips, as she thought Cromwell a terrible "baddy". She was an ardent fan of Stanley Baldwin, then Prime Minister, and as we more or less lived in the shadow of his home ground, we had to be frightfully deferential to him.

Teacher's loyalty to King and country knew no bounds, and I suppose to a certain extent this brushed off on us children. The abdication of Edward VIII (later Duke of Windsor) shattered our world completely. It was a huge and dreadful crisis and we all despised Mrs Simpson. At school, the children sang a skit on a well known song of the time, 'Organ Grinder Pete':

Who's that coming down the street?
Mrs Simpson, ain't she sweet
She's been married twice before
Now she's knocking on Edward's door.

We also sang:

Hark the herald angels sing
Mrs Simpson's pinched our King
Peace on earth and mercy mild
Is she going to have a child?
Joyful all ye nations rise
Listen to the people's cries
Pleased as man with man to dwell
Has she pinched the crown as well?
Hark the herald angels sing
Mrs Simpson's pinched our King!

A popular entertainer on the B.B.C., John Rourke, while singing 'Boiled Beef and Carrots' added at the end of the chorus "Oh! Mrs Simpson, pom – pom." He was quickly hustled off the air, and not allowed back on the radio for some months.

Women became very emotional about the whole business. I think it was probably because the King was a bachelor and they all saw themselves as potential Mrs Simpsons. The day the King abdicated, I had to go to hospital for an X-Ray. A man from the village remarked to my mother: "Amy was-a-blubberin' like a babby and I had a lump in me throat as big as a turnip!" I think that summed up the feelings of all. Certainly, most of the country wept for him. The King as Prince of Wales had been the blue-eyed boy favourite of all classes.

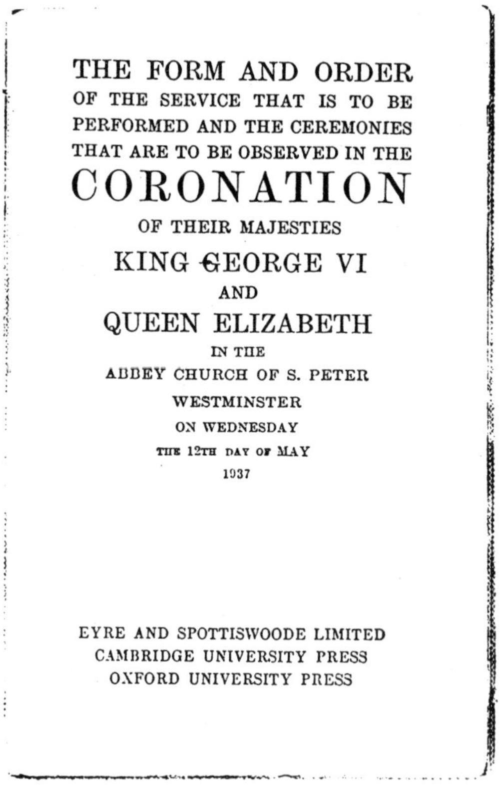

THE FORM AND ORDER
OF THE SERVICE THAT IS TO BE PERFORMED AND THE CEREMONIES THAT ARE TO BE OBSERVED IN THE

CORONATION

OF THEIR MAJESTIES

KING GEORGE VI

AND

QUEEN ELIZABETH

IN THE
ABBEY CHURCH OF S. PETER
WESTMINSTER
ON WEDNESDAY
THE 12TH DAY OF MAY
1937

EYRE AND SPOTTISWOODE LIMITED
CAMBRIDGE UNIVERSITY PRESS
OXFORD UNIVERSITY PRESS

We cheered up however at the imminent Coronation of George VI and celebrated with gusto at the Village Hall. We children had sports in a nearby field and there were events like bowling for the pig, egg and spoon races, apple dipping and the greasy pole. The latter consisted of a long pole that was greased and laid horizontally. To compete, people were timed to see how long they could stay on the pole – a task both difficult and dirty as they frequently slipped off onto the grass. Many a wife and mother had reason to curse that pole and the grass-stained clothes it gave rise to.

On this occasion we were all presented with Coronation mugs by the Lady who lived at the nearbye castle. We walked up to her and curtsied. Her daughter was standing with a large open box of chocolates; we each took one and curtsied again. The kids of today would expect a whole box, I suppose.

Then there was tea in the hall: nothing fancy, just paste sandwiches, jelly and a lovely cake in the shape of a crown with large pearls around the rim. Some lucky children also got a pearl for a keepsake. After tea was cleared, there was dancing and singing in the hall. Our current baker (no pun intended) sang with a dance band; we called him George Elrick. His name really was George and he looked somewhat similar to George Elrich who was a popular crooner of the time, not so much a romantic singer as Al Bowley or Sam Browne, but he sang jolly songs which everyone liked. I think he was with Henry Hall's band.

The men had a go, as well. My father, hanging drunkenly round the neck of our postman, sang, "Dear old pals, jolly old pals," and we sang "Daisy, Daisy, give me your answer, do" – I always used to wonder what an "answerdo" was. We also sang "It's a long way to Tipperary", and I wondered what a "rary" was and where they were going to tip it. It was years before I cottoned on to the truth!

Of course, we were all well-versed in pageantry. Two years

before, at the Jubilee of George V, we had celebrated in a like-fashion and been presented with Jubilee medals. The King made a speech on the wireless to us children saying: "When you grow up, you will be citizens of a Great Empire." We didn't need to be told that, we knew.

Armistice Day was treated with similar reverence; we were near enough in time to that great and terrible war for our parents to make sure of this, and some older people would go as far as to dress from head to toe in black, out of respect for their lost loved ones. If 11th November (Armistice day) fell on a school day, our two minute silence at eleven o'clock was always acted out in deadly seriousness.

One event that brought out the best – or the worst – in our loyalties, was the Heavyweight Championship of the World that took place between Joe Louis and Tommy Farr. I remember us strutting round the playground in groups, chanting loyal slogans in favour of Tommy Farr – though, secretly, I preferred Joe Louis, as I thought him better looking, being all shiny, smooth-skinned and black; a negro was a great novelty to our village in those days as we had never seen one in "real life" and were not to do so until the war came, and with it the black Americans.

In fact, anyone from outside Great Britain was a rarity. There was an inoffensive little Irishman named Daniel Raffity, who came over annually to work on the farm. He looked like everyone's idea of an Irishman, fresh from the potato famine. As he creaked by the playground on his rusty old bike, wearing a short jacket, tight trousers, leggings, a peculiar flat cap, and tiny steel-rimmed glasses, we would rush out to stare and stare at him. I think we were secretly frightened of him and regarded him as children of today might a spaceman from Mars.

I suppose loyalties took on a different aspect after the war. Children now adore footballers and pop stars, not Royalty, as we did. I used to have a big scrap-book into which I pasted all my photos and cuttings of the Royal Family: King George sitting on a model train, the Prince of Wales going down a coal mine; the Duke of Kent's lovely wedding to Princess Marina – a fairy tale romance if ever there was one. I also had a section for foreign Royalty. I was nutty about King Zog of Albania, a handsome, moustachiod monarch who looked every bit the romantic hero. I remember when he married young Queen Geraldine, I was madly jealous and ready to blow my juvenile brains out. Queen Geraldine later had a baby son; then they all had a revolution and got turned out of their country. It was awful for me! I later transferred my affection to King Farouk of Egypt who I thought was quite presentable as a young man. I was very bitter that neither of them ever saw and fell as madly in love with me. Forgive my romantic meanderings, I was only a sickly eight years old at the time.

CHAPTER 8

TRADESPEOPLE

Ours was a great neighbourhood for nick names. Most people at some time or other have been blessed or otherwise with something other than their legal baptismal name. My own paternal grandfather was known as "Poet" – nothing to do with his literary talents, rather on account of his regular emptying of the "po" several times nightly, watched in the bushes by concealed village boys. Since he had bred a family of thirteen and probably only possessed one "po", this seemed a logical thing to do.

We have had Tuckers, Chalkies, Badgers and Diggers, Spodges, Dobbies, Big Sams and Little Sams, Old Johns and Young Johns, Soap and Water, The man who was unkind to his mother, Farmer One Cow, and Miss Piddle Quick (self-explanatory). We've had Soddin' Sid, A Couple-a-Ducks, Mrs Thin Legs, The Man Who Causes A Dust Up At The Whist Drives, The Kaiser, The One Who Licks His Fingers, and Billy Allen's Double. A fellow up the road even referred to his father as "Our Old Woman's Old Man". There was also "Cabbage", so called because of the fact that he ate nothing but, and was usually to be found behind bushes, the cabbage having had an adverse effect on his bowels.

Another, a man called "The Toff", drove by every night and morning in a Rolls Royce, looking very aloof and neither to left or right. One day a neighbour out on his bicycle, found a tree fallen across the road. As The Toff was due to come along the road shortly, the neighbour waited, and stopped him to give warning of the tree. "How dare you stop me!" barked The Toff, and drove on with nose in the air. "Wished I'd let the old b . . . crash," said the neighbour. People like The Toff just behaved in that way and ordinary people were not expected even to look at them. Funny that, The Toff travelled our childhood roads for years and years, but we never knew who he was, or where he came from.

The Man Who Causes A Dust Up At The Whist Drives, was so called because one of our friends happened to say one night as he cycled by: "Oh! There's the man who causes . . . etc." Ever after ,we set our clocks by him. It'd be: "Let's see, it was just after The Man Who Causes A Dust Up At The Whist Drives went by." Or – "Your dad's late! The Man Who Causes A Dust Up At The Whist Drives went by some time ago."

Most of our tradespeople had nicknames. There was Foxy Woxy (the butcher), Laurence Of Arabia (the paper man), Mrs Taylor (the paper boy), Nevil The Devil (the baker), plus the aforesaid baker, George Elrick.

Then there were the coal men, Darkie, Coughy and Warty; Coughy so called because as he heaved the last cwt of coal off the lorry, he would suddenly develop nothing less than a grave yard cough, which sent my compassionate mother hurrying to make him a hot drink.

Another of our butchers, who came out from the town once a week, was just referred to as "Ernie"; his claim to fame was that his sister-in-law had given birth to quads – quite an accomplishment in those days.

As I mentioned before, we were very fond of our tradesmen. My mother liked Foxy Woxy the butcher, very much. He was a young fellow with a bright red neck. He used to come on Saturdays, and would stay for about an hour to drink tea and tell Mother all his troubles. One day, when talking about his own mother, he said with an emotional gulp: "I loved every hair of her head." Well, that may seem a normal remark to make, but put yourself in the place of a young child – there I sat on the floor behind his chair, trying to work out how it was possible to love every single hair on a person's head. I stared up at Foxy Woxy who had a thick head of black hair, and was very puzzled. Love to me meant being cuddled on my mother's knee, or my Auntie Annie's ample bosom. The thought of cuddling every one of Foxy Woxy's mother's hairs was beyond me.

We liked one of our bakers a lot, too. His name was Billy Bourne and when we handed him the bread book, he'd say:

"That's the chap that married Anna,

Sold her to buy a grand Piano."

On weekends he would dress up to the nines in plus-fours and a matching tweed cap and ride about the country side on a low-handle-barred sports bike. He was very stylish.

Darky was the first coal man I remember – I think I was about four. He was a cheeky young chap and one day when Mother, wearing a silk blouse fastened down the front by one of the new fashion zips, went out to pay him, he said: "What ever's that?" giving it a sharp pull. Down came the zip, revealing Mother's high-necked vest and petticoat. Was she embarrassed! –so, for a wonder, was Darkie! What a thing to happen in those days.

Although there were four grocery shops in the village, for years we took advantage of a weekly delivery service from town. Every Tuesday, Mr Parker would come pedalling furiously all the way from town, to collect our grocery order, and Mother would feel terribly sorry for him. He was painfully thin and wore a too-large overcoat, a too-large trilby hat which fitted over his ears, and bicycle clips on his thin legs. He was very servile, and bowed and scraped away at the back door. Dad always said: "Don't ask him in or you'll never get rid of him." So poor Mr Parker had to stand on the door step. Dad was probably right as there was such competition for custom that grocers and butchers would try every guile to sell extra goods. And Mr Parker was so thin, Mother would probably have been persuaded into buying all sorts of things she didn't really want and couldn't afford. He probably also had a widowed mother lined up, to say nothing of a wife and starving kids. Mr Taylor, the owner of the grocery shop, delivered the goods on Friday afternoon in time for tea and I'm sure Mother longed to ask him to pay Mr Parker more money – I think she likened him to Bob Cratchitt. Mr Taylor had a good singing voice and on high days and holidays would give us a song: "Hey Ho, come to the fair," he'd bellow out, to our delight.

The trouble with my mother being so kind-hearted, she could never refuse to buy things. At one time we had three bakers, two grocers, two butchers and two coal men, all calling at the house regularly, which for a family of four was a bit much!

The worst embarrassment was when they all called at the same time; for example, if both coal men turned up, Mother would have to have a cwt off each. While the one was being dealt with, the other would scowl, making disparaging remarks like: "You don't want to have any coal off him, it's full of rubbish." I used to skulk behind Mother's skirt, sensing her embarrassment and blushing for her. But it was no good, she just couldn't refuse them. "Poor beggar," she'd say, and give them our old clothes, or home-made cake and rice puddings for their children.

Of course nowadays, if we shop in town we get a lot more choice, but it isn't the same as having people call at the house. Some days it seemed like one long procession from morning till night. We didn't mind: it made an interest in our uneventful lives to listen to all their stories and grievances.

On Saturdays, at about eight o'clock in the evening, the butcher came with the Sunday Joint and 1lb of sausages. It was unthinkable then to keep uncooked meat for more than a day so we had the sausages for Saturday's supper. The butchers delivered everything; even a piece of liver guaranteed a visit and a cup of tea.

One of the best things about dealing with all these people was that at Christmas time we got gifts off them, or really lovely calenders. One baker used to give us books advertising *Jacob's Christmas Cakes* in colour. I used to cut out the prettiest cakes and "feed" them to my cut-out dolls. Running through the books was a condensed version of Charles Dickens'*A Christmas Carol* – that was my first brush with the story and how fascinating I found it.

Gifts of calenders, sometimes a Christmas pudding, a 1lb of butter or a tin of tea, used to tip the scales in favour of one or other of the tradespeople: "Well, they did give that lovely tin of biscuits," Mother would say, making up her mind. Or – "Pity, that was such a nice calender we had off them last year," deciding to dispense with their services in future.

One other tradesman who kept us ticking over, and brightened our lives considerably, was the travelling oilman. To call him an oilman is a bit of a laugh – makes him sound like Red Adair, which he wasn't for sure! It would be more precise to call him a pedlar, I suppose.

We used to have oil lamps for our lighting then: people would buy about two gallons of paraffin a week, more if they had one of the old round Aladdin stoves, and some would actually cook on these. We mainly cooked on the fire grate, with the oven which accommodated meats, puddings, baked potatoes and the firewood. Even stone hot water bottles were put in the oven to warm.

The oilman had a large open-sided van, with tarpaulin to cover over when it rained. He came once a week, bringing paraffin, candles, matches, wicks, accessories for lamps, crockery, shoe and furniture polish, *Brasso*, soaps, *Rinso* and *Persil* washing powders, *Zebra* black lead for grates, soda, *Jeyes* fluid, mats and carpets; with brushes, brooms, shovels, tin baths and buckets, clattering away on top of the van. What a treasure trove when he lifted off the tarpaulin!

We really looked forward to his visits, particularly when Mother was going to buy new cups; she usually had a surfeit of saucers, so she only bought odd cups, but we didn't mind, it was so exciting. You could buy carpets for a shilling a week on a club card. We also bought a lot of coconut matting and linoleum – or oilcloth as Mother still calls it to this day.

As Monday was cold meat, fried potatoes, the smell of washing, boiling in the copper, Mother with a woolly hat jammed over her ears, two cardigans and a pair of Dad's socks on (it was cold in the wash house); so Wednesday was "looking out for the oilman day", and making sure of remembering every odd household thing that was needed.

Finally, there was our postman, the lovely old Mr Crane. He used to stir his tea by running the spoon round and round the rim of the cup, gulping it down with a big slurp and finishing off by wiping and mopping up his large moustache.

One day he brought a letter, seemingly addressed to little me, which I opened eagerly and found wasn't; he had mistaken the name on the envelope. I cried bitterly, and Mr Crane gave me a new penny and promised to bring me a proper letter next day, which he did, but how he managed it, I can't think!

CHAPTER 9

AND OTHERS

On the corner of the road, not far from our house was a little wooden hut: this was Miss Shepherd's shop. Miss Shepherd lived in the back room and sold sweets in the front. How she made a living, it's hard to imagine. She only stocked about ten different varieties of sweets; she also owned about sixteen different varieties of cats! Miss Shepherd was old, thin and as frail as a piece of paper. She pinned her hair up on top, wore high collared blouses, with a Victorian brooch at the neck and long skirts to the floor. She was always trembly and looked spotlessly clean, though Mother didn't like us to go there for sweets because of the cats. When you asked for a quarter of humbugs, Miss Shepherd had to remove a tabby cat from the box in which they were kept. A black tom sprawled all over the fondants and a ginger and white lay on top of the butter drops. Requests for sherbet dabs brought about the removal of a black female, while numerous kittens, of all ages and sizes, played happily with the *Liquorice All-Sorts* batting them to and fro with cute little paws. "They don't like being disturbed," Miss Shepherd would say, reproving us in her gentle trembly voice, and we'd creep out, with our penny worth of sweets, feeling suitably ashamed.

Next to Miss Shepherd's shop was the farm. There, in a scruffy little room also called the "shop", the baker left hundreds of hot loaves, stacked on the old settle seat, reaching up to the ceiling and sprawling over the counter. These were for the weekend campers to whom the farm used to sell bolts of straw to sleep on (sixpence – 2½p – a bag), as well as bread and milk. Sometimes when we were short of bread we were sent down to the farm to ask if they could spare a loaf. This usually entailed a wait of an hour or more while the farmer, his wife, his wife's sister, his mother-in-law, the pig man and cow man (complete with dung and wellies) and anyone else who happened to be there, all poked their heads around the door and enquired: "Were we wanting something?" When we answered: "Mother said could they spare us a loaf?" the head in question would look worriedly behind and say: "I'll go and see." So on we waited till the next head poked round the door, with the same query and worried expression. And so it went on and on, until the sister-in-law, who was the big noise in the business, came out and told us that she could spare Mother half a loaf, hoped we were all well and that we would be careful of the traffic. Then, taking a loaf from the mountainous pile of hot bread, she would take it out the back to cut in half. This involved a further wait of perhaps half an hour, while more heads appeared worriedly round the door to enquire if we wanted something. You would have thought it was the Mafia calling, instead of two timid little girls!

Round the lane, about half a mile away from us, stood a black and white cottage – also a shop. This was owned by Mrs Gould who sold such items as tea, sugar, tobacco and sweets. There were a lot of these little cottage shops around the lanes. They'd have a shaky notice outside stating that they were licensed to sell tobacco. There were other notices nailed on the outside walls and stuck in the hedges: *Black Bell Tobacco, Black Cat Cigarettes, Wild Woodbines, Players Please, Craven 'A', Gold Flake* – all the popular brands of the time.

The shops were usually kept by elderly ladies. If you were lucky, you managed to catch them before they set off down their long gardens to feed the hens or some other task that took them away from the house. Sometimes they weren't there at all: they'd locked up and gone to market in Kidderminster and you'd have a wasted journey.

These shops had flexible hours; you could quite easily find them open at seven in the morning, or just as easily ten at night. It was purely a matter of luck, or your stars being in the right quarter.

Mrs Gould had a pony and trap and occasionally went into town, so if you heard her trit-trotting around the lane and noticed that she was dressed in her black coat and man's trilby hat, you knew there was no use in going to the shop.

These little shop keepers all worked on the same principle: the door stood open at all times. The "shop" consisted simply of a wooden counter that barred the entrance to the kitchen, and you'd have to stand there and wait until they decided to serve you. Eventually they would waddle slowly out and when you asked for a quarter of tea, they looked mighty suspicious, saying they'd see, or wait a minute, they just had to put the dinner on, or they just had to finish the washing up. We never minded, we weren't rushing madly around as we do today.

The nicest thing about walking home from school was that we could pass Mrs Cheshire's shop by the side of the bridge. Mrs Cheshire was plump, homely and smiley and so was her daughter who assisted her. They both had gingery-blonde hair. The shop sold wonderful things for children, although it was primarily there for the day trippers and visitors: sweets, dolls of every description – including the popular "Diddums" doll, balls in all sizes and colours, cricket bats, tennis rackets, straw hats and parasols. Oh! it was a fairy land of splendour to walk around the little veranda and gaze at these lovely things. You could buy a diamond or ruby ring for sixpence. If we had any birthday money we often spent it there; Mrs Cheshire and daughter never minded how long we gazed or how much time we wasted, they were completely unhurried and relaxed.

My favourite shop of all was at the most northerly point of the village. Usually called the "top shop" because of its position, it involved a walk of about four miles there and back, so we only went about once a month. The shop was always full of people, all chattering and gossiping. You could buy shoes and sandals, dress material, wool, blouses and skirts, stockings and socks, laces, ribbons, buttons, pins and needles, towels, pillowcases, writing paper; there was almost nothing that Mrs Sanders didn't stock, and if she didn't she'd soon order it for you.

She was another calm and unhurried shopkeeper. I used to gaze at her with adoration, and longed to be just like her when I grew up; so much so that after a visit to the shop, I would play at "being Mrs Sanders" with my dolls. She was a good-looking woman, neat and tidy, with beautiful smooth skin and soft hair which she plaited around her ears. Her appearance was always immaculate. I most admired the way she had of doing up parcels. She'd spin them round and round on the counter while she folded the brown paper and tied the string, chatting away all the time. When finished, the parcels were perfect. A machine couldn't have done them better.

One day, when I was quite small, lolling on Mother's skirt and drooling admiringly as usual, a customer muttered something to Mrs Sanders, who, mounting the familiar step ladder, fetched down from the very top shelf an interesting little brown parcel, tied with string. The woman, blushing scarlet, whispered something about – "Always useful to have in the house" – snatched the parcel off the counter and shoved it well down inside her bag, covering it up with the other packages. Mrs Sanders calmly agreed on the usefulness of this article and the woman hurried out of the shop, looking neither to left or right in her embarrassment.

I was intrigued and asked my mother if I could have a parcel like that to undo. I think I imagined it was part of Father Christmas' secret store. Mother was suitably embarrassed, said she didn't know what it was, and hastily changed the subject. I brooded for some time about this, until it eventually went out of my mind. This was my unconscious introduction to sanitary towels. A taboo subject, of course.

Another little commercial enterprise invaluable to locals, was the village dressmaker. There in their front parlours, away from the prying eyes of menfolk, these ladies stitched and pinned and fashioned and fitted to get garments suitably right for the individual. People "made do" and cared for their clothes then; and dressmakers would turn collars and cuffs, or even turn and re-stitch a whole dress or coat in order to give them many years of wear.

Auntie Bo once had a dress made at our dressmakers. What a palaver it was! The long walk to her house, the fittings, the taking teas with Miss Hesketh! But new clothes were exciting, being so few and far between. When finally the dress was ready, we all went to admire it. It was then placed in the tin trunk, packed in tissue paper and surrounded by lavender sachets and pieces of carbolic soap, until an occasion arose which Auntie Bo considered important enough to wear it.

Mother was always trying to make a bit of extra money by selling bits and pieces. We had always sold garden produce: our sixpenny bunches of sweet peas, the three-penny button holes for the men and Mother's half a crown Saturday mixed flowers were well-known in the camping field; so she tried her hand at other products. *Malvona* tomatoes were a good line and so were cigarettes. Whenever a new brand came out, we used to advertise it on large sticky posters on either side of the cottage wall. One amusing poster consisted of a bald-headed infant named Henry, hurrying along with a balloon coming from his mouth, saying: "Henry says . . . cigarettes are best." It amused us children and a few-passers by, but didn't improve the sale of the cigarettes at all!

The most popular line we had was Mother's homemade ice cream. This was gorgeous stuff, made with ice cream powder. The method was: mix the ice cream powder with a little milk and a pinch of salt, add boiling milk until it looked like custard, then churn it round and round until it was thick enough to be put in a container packed around with cooling ice. It was a great success while it lasted. We only sold it on Sundays, when the campers and weekenders came. They rolled up with basins, cups and jugs to buy it loose, or bought penny (½p) cornets or two penny (1p) wafers.

Our ice cream could only be sold by courtesy of Sid and Charlie. These two were the driver and conductor of our local bus, which drove every Saturday into town. The old bus would come pop-banging up the road at about ten in the morning and park in the lane. Sid, the conductor, would stroll down and pick up a wooden bucket to collect the ice. Then off they went, Charlie parping on the horn, chugging away with a bus-load of passengers. When they came back in the afternoon to return the bucket, they were given cups of tea while their passengers waited outside in the bus and Mother hastily put the ice bucket in the pantry, which was the coldest part of the house. Then away went the bus with Charlie puffing on his pipe, blowing the horn, the passengers waving and Sid hanging precariously by one foot on the running board, also waving, until they were out of sight.

Another lovely personal service Sid and Charlie used to offer was to turn down old narrow lanes and drop elderly people at their doorstep, or deliver parcels en route. Can you wonder we mourn the passing of those times?

Sid and Charlie – another pair of country characters. With Sid's round, red face and Charlie's long, white one, it was inevitable their nick-names became Orange and Lemon.

I suppose all country places have their characters. We certainly had ours. There was the old man who washed his feet in *Jeyes'* fluid; the woman who put her babies' nappies in the oven to air, and wasn't satisfied with the results until they turned a pale brown; up the bank was old Charlie who lived quite happily in a derelict pig sty; and Boatlay Jack who shacked up with poor little bent old Hannah in an old Birmingham tram by the river. Up the road from us was a dear little cottage, very tiny even by country standards. The family who lived in it were exceptionally tall, and it was reputed that the son had to sleep with his feet hanging out of the bedroom window, owing to the lack of space. Another of our neighbours was a real hypochondriac (although we didn't realise it at the time). She always had something the matter with her and was very proud of it. She'd come cringing down the road, shoulders hunched, head bowed in anguish, moaning all the way: "Oh! I be bad," she'd say. (We kids used to make fun of her behind her back and say: "Oh! I pea pod," – because that's what it sounded like.) Then she would get talking and would soon be shrieking with laughter, forgetting her ailments, as she really was a jolly person at heart.

In the mornings she worked at the local pub. The landlord's sons held a sweep-stake among the employees, sixpence a go, on what would be the matter with her each day. They had a chart worked out for the draw, with categories for stomach, back, arms, legs, bowels, kidneys, head, ears, feet and so on. As is often the case with hypochondriacs, she really was a robust woman. She was always creeping down to Mother declaring that she had been sitting in the lavatory in a dead faint for half an hour. I doubted if she had ever fainted in her life and so did the doctor. Mrs Pea Pod was a good old soul, with a kind heart and true neighbourliness, but she did so love her little performances.

Darkie was an old fellow who came every year at pea-picking time to assist the farmer and help supervise the pickers. He was a coloured man and told us he had been born in Jerusalem: he was very proud of this fact. At one time he had done some boxing. His poor old wrists had been broken so often, they seemed to turn the wrong way when you were following behind him: with his dark face and neck, his cap pulled down over his eyes, and these strange wrists, he looked like he was walking backwards with his feet the wrong way. He had some puppet dolls, with which he used to entertain the visitors, giving a boxing match and commentary. When I first remember him, he was doing the big Jack Johnson fight. Then he progressed to Tommy Farr and Joe Louis, and the last I saw of him, it was Bruce Woodcock. Wonder if he ever got to Mohammed Ali? The puppets all looked the same. Darkie just changed their grubby shorts around, dabbed extra paint on their faces and they became whomever he wanted them to be.

We had a few famous characters, too. The Aston Villa football team, for instance, came for a six weeks' training course in the orchard down the road. They used to belt past our house every morning on their run. Knees up, arms akimbo, "Knees up, Mother Brown," we'd shout. The ladies in the neighbourhood were very excited and enamoured with them and loved to watch them running by. We kids just thought they were daft. Their knees were too knobbly and ugly. Football wasn't the religion it is today and we didn't often see men in shorts, anyway.

As we lived not far away from the Shelsley Walsh hill climb track, we also had racing drivers visiting our area in the summer. Raymond Mays and Sir Malcolm Campbell were two. If we were lucky they gave us a wave as they passed by.

CHAPTER 10

SUPERSTITIONS AND FANTASIES

Like most country districts, we had our words and sayings peculiar to us.

We had harchetecs (architects), we had liars (lawyers). Some of us drank *Typhoid* tea, some of us had coronations (carnations) blooming in our gardens, to say nothing of gladiators (gladioli); others ate dinner with prongs (forks). During the war, our next door neighbour was full of praise for the brave Cretoslovaks fighting Hitler.

Old Mr Green donned his flush-floors (plus-fours) every Sunday and made his way down to the bridge to see which way the river was-a-flowin'. Quite a few of the villagers were moor-hens (morons) and most of us were descended from pheasants (peasants).

No doubt we were a funny lot. Some had thin blood, others thick skins. We had colds in our eyes, stomachs and backs; we had gumboils. If we fell down in the playground, we got gravel rash. If our eye twitched they said we were "making blood"; while white spots on the finger nails, or ulcers on the tongue meant that we had been telling lies. When we cut a finger we dabbed it with peroxide and if the peroxide bubbled, we said: "Ah! It's going septic", and proceeded to swathe it in a large bandage, until all the poison had gone. I've since learnt that peroxide bubbles anyway. Amen to that!

Some days we were "alright", some days we were "fair to middlin'". And we knew that Cuckoos didn't leave us to fly south in the autumn, they changed into hawks.

We had inexplicable sayings like: "My word, it's black over Bill's mother's," – who was Bill? And – "You look like a dying duck in a thunder storm!"

"Come in if you're fat, stay out if you're thin," my mother used to say. She also had a saying about Pershore, she said: "Pershore, God help us."

I later discovered this originated from the times when Pershore people depended on plums for a livelihood; if there was a bad crop, they said: "We come from Pershore, God help us."

When wirelesses started to be popular, grown-ups listened avidly to every weather forecast. One mother dragged her unwilling off-spring up to the doctor's surgery saying: "He's got a deep depression coming over." She didn't add: "from Iceland", but that's what she meant. I think this was more a case of the mother suffering from radioitis.

If we wanted to do something in particular, we'd be told: "You can do it just now", which should have meant "just now", but didn't; it meant later – which was very confusing to strangers in the district.

People were always telling us "things". Teacher told us that Dutch people were so clean they washed the outside of their houses every day (I can only suppose that they must have been wooden houses). While the Dutch were busy washing the outside of their houses, the Bristolians were washing their "puddies" (hands), the Lancastrians their "donnies", and we in the Midlands were doing the same to our "dannies".

"Don't you drink that icy cold water straight from the well, Jocelyn," said Mrs Daniells, "or you'll drop down dead." Grown-ups seemed bent on frightening the life out of us.

"I knew a man once," said Mrs Passey, "who got an earwig in his ear; it went in one ear and come out of the other, that's why they are called earwigs. Of course," she added, "it killed him."

"I knew a chap what catched a frog in the 'ay field, and swallered it live, to get rid of his asthma," said Mr Wood.

"The one ambition of a bat, is to get in ladies' hair," said someone else.

"You mustn't knit, sew or play cards or games on Sunday," said another, "or God will strike you down."

We never ate bananas (bad for the digestion) unless crushed with sugar and milk; or cucumber and we never ate tinned salmon. We never ate *any* tinned food except on very special occasions, such as the visit of a towny Aunt and Uncle, and then only fruit or sardines and only *Skippers' Sardines*, which were trustworthy – like the healthy jolly old sailor man on the paper wrapping. (They didn't actually say the last bit but I have a feeling that's what they meant!)

We were also told never to touch berries, unless they were legitimate blackberries growing in the country side (sound advice). I can never look a deadly nightshade in the stamen to this day, since, as a trembling child, I first encountered this fearsome terror – even if avoiding its sneering beckoning stance meant a sidle all around the hedgerows.

When folk talked of putting money in the bank, I envisaged a mossy bank with violets growing, and sensible people with contented sensible smiles, poking shillings and sixpences deep into its grassy slopes. This idea probably arose on account of my hearing that a local boy had stolen some money and buried it in the garden. The boy got the cruel birch for his crime.

On the subject of punishments, I should mention here that Auntie Bo had her own methods of dealing with dishonesty. If she caught a child taking plums or apples off the trees, or anything out of the garden, she marched them into the back kitchen, washed their grubby faces and hands in carbolic soap, wiped their runny noses, gave them a piece of bread and jam, a halfpenny and told them never to do it again. They didn't!

We believed that a red sky at night was a shepherd's delight. When the wind was in the east "t'was neither good for man nor beast", and when the peacock loudly bawled, then it was time to "expect rain and squalls".

We fed our colds and starved our fevers. We never turned feather beds on Fridays (unless we were really brave like Auntie Bo). If we broke a mirror we didn't dare tell an adult as it would have caused them too much worry. If a picture fell off the wall, it was a sign of death and we were steeped in foreboding for weeks. If we dropped a glove or a knife, we never picked it up for fear of the dire consequences; we had to wait around until someone came to oblige, maybe one of our friendly tradesmen.

When we peeled an apple we tried to get the peel complete and unbroken, then we tossed it over our left shoulder. It was supposed to fall into the shape of the initial of the man we were going to marry – many a girl's expectations were ruined by this!

If two people said the same thing in unison, they linked little fingers and made a secret wish. Then they said the name of a poet or author, like Shakespeare or Burns, the first that came into their head, and that made the wish come true.

If we saw a pin we picked it up "then all day we had good luck". When we laughed before breakfast "we cried before night".

On Twelfth Night (Epiphany) we burned the holly and mistletoe in the chimney to get rid of evil spirits – the same holly that we had not dared to bring indoors until 24th December (are people today with central heating possessed by evil spirits, we ask ourselves?) When a child had a nose bleed, Teacher put the big porch key down its back; and the wooden ruler under the tongue of a child having a fit.

Heavy thunder meant that God was having some coal delivered in Heaven. One would have thought it more logical for Satan to order coal, but never mind that, it cheered us up. People were terrified of thunder and lightening, and hurried to cover up mirrors and knives with cloths. Children weren't allowed to play or even speak during a storm; we were usually too busy silently praying !

One of the jolliest superstitions we found, on holiday in Portsmouth, was touching the sailors' collars for luck. With the thousands of sailors walking about in the evenings, we soon tired of trying to touch every one. I'll never forget how cheerful and jolly those sailors seemed to be. They were a colourful sight on Southsea front at night, milling everywhere, their blue and white uniforms standing out against the background of the illuminations and the flower gardens. It was exciting to us children, who had never seen any uniforms before the war came. We longed to live by the sea and were told peculiar stories about how the seven creases in the uniform trousers represented the seven oceans of the world; and the black ribbons worn around the neck were a token of mourning for Lord Nelson – sailors could only remove them at their weddings, at which time they were substituted for white ones.

Many other things we were told, but I have, alas, forgotten them!

CHAPTER 11

BEAUTY AND SEX

When I was a child, I craved for a piano, a teddy bear coat, a tortoise, long golden curls, blue eyes, short legs, a small mouth and a beautiful smile. We had no room for a piano, no cash for a teddy bear coat, and no parental enthusiasm for a tortoise. As I was already equipped with black hair, hazel eyes, long hairy legs and a large mouth, to say nothing of hairy arms, eyebrows that would put Groucho Marx to shame and a scowl, you can imagine the frustrations I underwent in my efforts to become a beauty. To add to all these misfortunes, I had an ugly ganglion lump the size of a bantam's egg on my left wrist and black circles under my eyes similar to a panda's, except that pandas hadn't been invented then.

As I grew older, I learned to get by with a little help from my friends – my friends being, once again, good old *Reckitt's Blue*, which I used to rinse my hair in, having been thus informed and advised by a magazine. "Turn a deaf ear to expensive shampoos," said the mag., "and rinse your lovely black hair with *Reckitt's Blue*." And *Veet*. The day I discovered *Veet* was the happiest day of my life. At last, here was a chance to become hairless! My hairy arms used to be a terrible embarrassment. Rolling jumper sleeves up for painting or modelling lessons at school – "Ooo, look at the hairs on your arms," my kindly friends would shout, accusingly. So one day, when I was about eleven, I managed to illicitly buy some *Veet*, a product which had just come on the market. I tried it on my arms. The hairs rolled off. It was glorious. I sat in the deck chair under the apple tree all that day, admiring my beautiful smooth skin. Nothing could hold me back now, the world was my oyster. I could be a famous film star and marry Ronald Coleman. Look out, Greta Garbo! Hollywood, Paris, Rome, Vienna lay ahead. Unfortunately, I hadn't reckoned on the hairs re-growing; the least said about that the better. Later on, I decided to shave my legs with Dad's cut-throat razor, bringing cries of alarm from my mother. Not only could I inflict a serious injury on myself, but what if I should be cast away on a desert island, without a razor? I should grow to look just like an ape! It was all very worrying for her.

The doctor had a go at the ganglion. He held my hand on the gate post, and hit it maliciously with a medicine bottle. Nothing happened! I was then advised by the old folks to try it with a family Bible. We didn't have a family Bible strong enough to even make a dent in it. One day it just disappeared. The hand swelled, the matter dispersed and the lump was never seen again.

Though my mother thought that we were beautiful children, my sister was convinced she was the ugliest girl in the world. I was convinced that I was. My legs were so thin, boys shouted: "Yah! Sparra' legs," at me. We didn't stand much of a chance of being beautiful in the Thirties, particularly in winter time. Winter wouldn't have been complete without chilblains, chapped hands, red noses and frozen faces. I don't care what the experts say, winters were colder then. We were colder.

Adults gave us no encouragement in our quest for beauty. "My word, isn't she pale and thin!" they'd say. And I'd be pale and thin to oblige them. It was like the Stanley Holloway song – 'My Word, You Do Look Queer'. They told me I didn't look well and I didn't feel well – so there!

In fact, it was probably more comfortable for me to be unwell, as I could then stay in bed. Some of my happiest childhood moments were spent lying in bed, reading, with a coal fire dancing in the little bedroom grate, the old wicker chair creaking – and not being expected to eat if I didn't want to. Many times I was just too terrified to go to school, and being "unwell" was my way of retreating from the rat race. I remember one day, when I was about twelve, my father and me were at an auction sale in the village; someone asked me how I was and, like the polite child I had been taught to be, I answered: "Very well, thank you." "Well, that's a change," they said. I was equally astonished at my answer. It was the first time I had been conscious of actually feeling well.

Looking glamorous was an up-hill struggle. We discovered that if we could rake up sixpence in stamps, the *Tokalon* cosmetic people would send us a box of all their trial-size products. Day cream, night cream and about six different powder shades in little sachets were included. Our mothers didn't mind this but they drew the line at lipstick – so we stuck to the old trick of rubbing our lips with red sweets. We looked *hateful*. Many a small girl had reason to bless the *Tokalon* firm. I imagine they must have done a roaring and uneconomical trade in those beauty boxes. Probably kept a staff specifically employed to send out thousands of them, the length and breadth of the British Isles. What a laugh!

One cosmetic our mothers actually liked – probably because they could buy it in the shop by the bridge, which was less complicated than sweating and pouring over a hot Woolworths' counter in town – was called *Phulnana*. It looked and smelt like custard powder. They adored it! They also loved *Californian Poppy* and *Ashes of Roses* perfume. Us children were partial to a dab of *Californian Poppy* – only one dab, mind. It was so expensive: sixpence a bottle! Our mother's ambition was to have a giant size for one shilling and eleven pence (9½p).

An *Amaimi* wave set and dinky curlers helped no end to make our hair less grotesque than we thought it was. Some girls had their hair done up by doting mothers in curl rags every night. I suppose they thought they would turn out looking like Shirley Temple. I was terribly jealous of such kids, and couldn't convince Mother that my life was being ruined by having straight hair and a fringe. After all, what did she know about it, being so old herself? We were Hollywood-orientated at an early age. In conversation, people were always referring to "the one with curly hair", or remarking on what beautiful ringlets so and so had, "just like Mary Pickford". It was all so frustrating.

Another beauty trick was to rub our legs with gravy browning to give the sun-tanned look. It wasn't very successful. The gravy used to run in the heat of the sun, and the flies had a whale of a time!

When I was eleven, my childhood ailments culminated in a magnificent swan song. Mother called in the doctor to lance a whitlow on my thumb, and he retaliated by announcing I had a strained heart. I had to spend the next six months in bed resting. This was splendid, until some thoughtless visitor remarked that I would grow more in bed. As I was then five feet, four inches, this came as a shattering blow. When I got up again, I would be a giant! And nobody would want to marry a freak! I had recovered from my love affairs with Kings Zog and Farouk by this time, but had fallen even deeper in love with Ronald Coleman, having recently seen *The Prisoner of Zenda* at the Silver Cinema in Worcester, in which he played the leading role. I also had a crush on Raymond Massey who appeared in the same film – a very unlikely hero for a young girl's passion. But if I was to go on growing, and these gentlemen perchance came walking along our road, I wouldn't stand a dog's chance of either falling madly in love at first sight with me – we ardently believed in love at first sight then; it was a desperate hope that we clung to!

When I arose from my sick bed, I wasn't a giant, but a weak, gangly, stooped girl, with an inferiority complex to match. My clothes neither fitted, nor suited me. My skirts were too straight to disguise my skinniness, and I had to turn the tops over double to keep them from hanging around my ankles. This created a bulge round my waist rather like a *Michelin* tyre. My feet were big and clumsy in flat school shoes, and my stockings eternally wrinkled around match-stick legs. I was a poor in-between. In fact, there never stood a between more in than me! Certainly no chance of romance with a Hollywood, or a Ruritanian prince, I sighed. Have to take a closer look to home.

My disgruntled eyes rested on Gordon. Why I chose him to develop a crush on, it's hard to say. He was no beauty – pug nose, protruding teeth, pop eyes, greasy hair, round shoulders. Small and pathetic Gordon passed by on his bicycle every night, delivering a quart of goat's milk from his boss to his boss's friend in the next village. He was no lady-killer and took no notice of me. With a wink and a jerk of his head, he used to shout out to a gang of us: "Turned out nice again!" – which he'd pinched off George Formby – or, "Warm again!" The answer to that catch-phrase, which we'd all shout with gusto, was: "Nice now!" I just had to hope the others hadn't noticed how red my face had become. Oh! It was ecstasy and agony to feel compelled – driven by powerful forces beyond me – to wait for the sight of Gordon every night!

After Gordon, there was Frank, a paper boy I fancied. Cycling from Droitwich to deliver a load of morning papers to the shop, he'd come flying down the hill, feet daringly on the handlebars and swoop like a giant swallow down the back lane. This Evil Kenevil of the Thirties was always accompanied by two smaller boys riding shot gun a little behind him, obviously adoring him from afar. He was so dashing, his hands seldom touched the handlebars and never the brake.

Sex was something that never reared its ugly head. We thought we were growing up into a beautiful romantic world. We never said "breast", or "midwife", or "nudity", which were classed as cheeky words; and ladies who were expecting babies, were expecting babies:

they were never pregnant. We learned to cleverly skate round certain words, using substitutes like "busk" measurements. A lady with a "female" problem had her "wound" removed. All very subtle. There was next to no vulgarity in our hearing. The rudest poem I ever came into contact with, was:

Red, white and blue,
There was a kangeroo
Who went behind a dustbin
To do his number two.

but I would never have dared to repeat this.

We were so lovely and innocent. "Fairies" were little people that only the privileged could see, or bits of thistledown that we chased on a summer breeze. Being "gay" meant being happy or jolly. "Camp" was either coffee that we drank (very occasionally) or a thing that boy scouts went to in summer.

A "Queen" was either "Mary" or "Elizabeth", "Consort of George VI", "Our British pride and joy", or else a bee that remained in the hive for unexplained reasons. We believed that a whistling woman and a crowing hen was neither good for God "nor men".

We did pure and innocent things, like going "primrosing" or "snowdropping"; eating hawthorn bread and cheese off the hedgerows; looking for pussy willow for Palm Sunday; or making miniature tea parties for our dolls in the garden, with stick furniture, flower heads for hats, and large leaves for sun shades. We didn't have pop stars, but we had pop flowers: little wild flowers, stitchwort, growing in the hedge rows in July which could be popped between fingers on the way to and from school. Gosh! We were nice.

I never knew anything about the production of babies. I only knew that a baby was a wet slobbery yellow or red creature, to be avoided at all costs. They screamed and cried and were often a nuisance to my school mates who were kept home from school to mind them while their mothers went out to work. Babies were always supposed to be loved and cherished by their brothers and sisters, who would never have dared to confess what they really thought of them.

Near to Grandad's house, lived a family named Dowells. In their meagre little cottage, with one room up and one down, Mrs Dowells was always having babies. When a new baby arrived, Auntie Bo, to impress a little of the facts of life upon us and "babies were gifts from God and weren't they all lovely" sort of idea, would drag us unwillingly round to see this new miracle of life. She would take a milk pudding for the poor mother and sixpence to press into the infant's hand. Mrs Dowells, looking ill and yellow, would be sitting up in bed in the downstairs room, with the little miracle wrapped in a piece of old blanket clutched to her yellow flabby bosom and all the other little Dowells standing proudly around the bed, wiping their runny noses on their sleeves. I was not impressed. Auntie Bo would seize the baby from Mrs Dowells' loving arms and jiggle it madly up and down, exclaiming what a delightful child it was, the prettiest she'd ever seen, but she hoped that it would be the last, as surely Mrs Dowells had enough children to cope with. Mrs Dowells would smile politely, but not optimistically. This procedure went on for many years and oncoming babies.

One day, when I was about twelve years old, there was a bit of a commotion at school. I learnt that a girl, Norah Collins, was going to "catch it" from Teacher when she came in.

The girl was bustled out into the porch and came back looking very pink and embarrassed. Teacher looked white and embarrassed. Word went round that Norah, who was also twelve, had been kept home from school to assist at the "birth" of one of her mother's numerous babies. Well, *I* didn't know what that meant. Most of us girls were ignorant, not all. At playtime we surrounded Norah; we were determined, though slightly apprehensive, to discover what had happened.

Norah was reluctant to say anything. The poor girl stood there trying to put us off: telling us that Teacher had said she would cane her if she repeated a single thing to the other girls and that she was to keep strictly silent on the matter.

Well, Norah was badgered and persuaded into parting with her information.

"But where do babies actually come from?" we persisted.

Scarlet-faced Norah eventually replied: "Out of yer behind!"

"Phaw!" we said, "What a tale, don't expect us to believe that, do you?"

"It's the truth," Norah spluttered.

"You're a liar, Norah Collins," we said, chased her round the playground and had no more to do with her, until she admitted that it couldn't possibly be true, that she must have made a mistake.

We relented and were friends with her again, but seeds of suspicion had been sown in our ignorant minds and life was never quite the same again. Poor Norah – and poor us!

CHAPTER 12

PLEASURES, PASTIMES AND OUTINGS

We were never "made" to go to church. This was strange: both our parents belonged to Christian families, and my mother's father had even been organist and sidesman at various churches.

We lived a good way from the churches in either village which meant a long walk in the dark in winter, and Mother was always busy with her selling in the summer, so perhaps that was the reason. I can't say that I was sorry, as I never found going to church very inspiring. Teacher often asked us on a Monday morning who had been to church, and it was nice to put my hand up with the rest of the sanctimonious bunch, but that was about its only redeeming feature.

We had a vicar who gabbled through the service at one church and a vicar who stuttered through at the other. The gabbler was really quite interesting, with a good sense of humour and very popular. He used to race his car madly through the village, in the same way that he raced through the sermon – scattering people to left and right. My father had a lift back from town with him one day, and staggered out of Vicar's car with more white hairs than he started out with. It took a good few glasses of homemade wine to calm his nerves!

So, I didn't like school and I didn't like church. What did I like? Well, I liked Paul Robeson, no, that's wrong; from the time of being a young infant I *loved* Paul Robeson. You remember Auntie Bo's gramophone? The greatest pleasure I had when staying with Auntie Bo, was to be allowed to hear my favourite records. The most glorious, to be kept until last, was 'Fat Little Fella With His Mammie's Eyes'. Wonderful! Paul Robeson was at his most popular at this time. Everyone admired his deep chocolate voice.

One day Mother bought from Worcester, 'Old Man River' as a present for Grandad. It was placed reverently on a chair. What a mistake! I came in, sat on it and broke it. Such a commotion you never did hear! We could have bought another for sixpence, but that didn't console me. I thought I had killed Paul Robeson.

When Auntie Bo poked the broken pieces into the garden (in those days people used broken 78s in their flower pots and gardens for drainage), I waited and waited, hoping another Robeson would grow out of the ground; like the genie from Aladdin's lamp, he would rise, tall and brown and wonderful. Thank heavens I really hadn't killed him, and was able to still love and enjoy him until recent years.

I also loved my dolls. My sister and I had a large variety, thanks to the generosity of Auntie Nellie's employers – many wealthy people adopted, in a sense, the families of their nannies and maids. The Koebels were very kind to us and always sent us lovely presents for Christmas and birthdays.

We used to have a lot of china dolls which we dressed in handmade clothes. I had a lovely one with real auburn hair – I named her Tessa. There was also Priscilla, Daphne, Jacko and Dinah, and "bless her heart".

Then there was my adored Teddy Bear. I had Teddy for my fifth birthday, and when I was a bit older, knitted him suits in red, white and blue stripes (patriotism, you'll remember). Teddy was later to change his sex and become Katherleen, when my small son took possession He also became hairless, eyeless and whiskerless. Little boys have no respect.

Sunny Jim was another great favourite. We got him free from saving up the coupons on the *Force Cereal* packet. He was a rag doll and took a fair amount of bashing around, as rag dolls do.

As well as our china dolls, we had many cut-outs. My sister, going through an artistic phase, used to design and cut them out of cardboard. The ladies would all have round, red cheeks, grotesque Cupid's bows, and perfect bosoms that stuck out of the sides of their bodies like water wings (that was a little bit saucy of my sister, I don't know how she dared!). They also had blond curls, of course, blue eyes and lashes that looked like park railings. The gentlemen had black, sleek hair, parted on the side, wore evening dress, and were all terribly, terribly handsome. They all looked like dance band leaders. Some of them wore spectacles, like Carrol Gibbons and my sister. She was a genius at designing their clothes. She made the ladies beautiful pink ball dresses and we had balls for them; they'd get up on the stage and sing songs like 'When My Dream-Boat Comes Home' and 'Red Sails In The Sun Set'.

My sister's cut-out family were the MacDonalds (she was going through her Scottish phase at the time – something to do with Ramsey MacDonald, I believe). There was Mr and Mrs Malcolm MacDonald, Maud MacDonald and her brother Jack. Maud MacDonald was a frightful prig. My family were the Fieldings – Mr and Mrs, Geoffrey Fielding, and Bluebell Fielding. Geoffrey was a bit of a wag and sang naughty songs at the balls, but was much admired for his spunk and grit, by the rest of the family.

My sister was a very good scholar. She won first prize – an assortment of *Cadbury's* chocolates – for writing an essay at school about the cocoa bean; she also won first prize in a painting competition – a fountain pen with a nine carat gold nib. Really, that was a bit of a fluke.

Every year, the *Oxo* company sent round painting books for children to colour the picture of their choice, always with a pen for the prize. The year my sister won, the pictures were of famous historical characters, and she chose Isaac Newton. Teacher's mother was to be the judge.

When the paintings were finished and laid out anonymously on the table, Teacher disappeared into her living quarters and reappeared, nervously prodding and shepherding her grumpy old mother towards the table. Grumpy old mother, having just been disturbed from her afternoon nap, took one look at the paintings, stabbed her bony finger at my sister's, which happened to be the nearest and beat a hasty retreat back to her arm chair, there to resume her slumbers.

We all clapped Teacher's absent mother and my sister, who blushingly went up to receive her prize. The silly thing was, we had one pupil who was an excellent artist and later went on to paint fine china at the porcelain works in Worcester. He was furious, coveting that pen as his right. We all laughed about it in later years.

On the strength of my sister's amazing success in the art and literary worlds, we persuaded her to enter the *Palm Toffee* competition. The prizes were wonderful – something like ten pounds for first prize. If she won, we'd be set up for life.

The poem she submitted went –

The cow, the country and the sun,
Makes Palm Toffee just A1.

– with a drawing of a bloated and imbecilic cow to accompany it. She didn't win a blind thing. That was the end of her career as an artist.

I was always sending away for "things" by post. I joined The Ovaltinies and The Cococubs and got all the badges and literature that accompanied membership of such prestigious clubs. We loved badges; I had one of Amy Johnson's aeroplane given to me. I also saved up fifty pictures of film stars out of *MilkyWay* packets and got a giant size photograph of Raymond Massey.

Another big thing in our lives was the collecting of cigarette cards. We had thousands: royalty, ships, dogs, garden flowers, wild flowers, radio stars, film stars. Film stars were the favourites and we'd devotedly learn all about who was married to whom in Hollywood. But by the time we'd sorted it all out, they'd be divorced and married to someone else! When Ronald Coleman wed Benita Hume, his second and last wife, I got her out of my "set" and gazed curiously at her. What did he see in her? She looked so ugly

VERY SECRET

—to be read

by Cococubs only

The

Cococubs

I AM A COCOCUB

CADBURY JON…

COCOCUBS

CADBURY

BOURNVILLE

Dear Cococub,

We are all so glad you have joined us, and welcome you as a full member of the Cococubs. The Badge is with this letter; boys should wear it on the left side of their coat or jersey, girls on the right.

Mind you read the rules in the booklet carefully, and learn the code and secret sign. When you know them, seal up the pages with the red seal so that people who are not Cococubs cannot read the secrets.

I do hope you will write to me and say how you like the club. If you have any suggestions about it let me know.

With best wishes,

Jonathan

to me – I nearly threw her away or swapped her, but the thought of spoiling the "set" stopped me. How I hated her.

We used to buy comics every week: *Rainbow* and later on, *Girls Own* and *The Dandy*. An old pal of my father's called every Sunday morning and left us *The Jester*, and others that his boys had finished with. *The Jester* never looked clean; whether this was because it was already a sort of sickly green, I can't say. Mother hated this old man because he swore so much and took my dad off to the pub. The minute he'd gone, she would put the comics into the oven to sterilise them. I think she thought we would catch something off them, maybe swearing and drinking! When they came out of the oven, they would be crisp and fragile, and *The Jester* a pale brown colour. We didn't care. We enjoyed them, crinkly and crackly as they were.

At school we played lots of games – another thing we actually enjoyed. 'The farmers in his den', 'As I was in the kitchen', 'Salt, mustard, vinegar, pepper' were all skipping games.

Sheep, sheep come home,
We are afraid,
What of – the wolf.
The wolf's gone to Lancashire
And won't be back for many a year,
So sheep, sheep, come home.

We didn't know where Lancashire was. We only knew that Gracie Fields lived there; still, at least we knew all about the grass lands of Tibet!

Another game we liked was called Statues. This involved being whirled round and round, then tossed, and however we fell, we had to stay in that position. No wonder we had gravel rash!

Once a year, during the summer term, we took a penny to school; this enabled us to watch the ventriloquist and his doll. The unlucky children who couldn't afford a penny, had to play outside, angrily and frustratedly kicking a ball around and trying to peep through the tall windows. The ventriloquist rode up on a tall, heavy, black bicycle. He had long black hair, long black moustaches, black finger nails, and he wore a long black coat with little caped shoulders, a black tie and black boots but no socks; and he had a long white face. He was a study in black and white, and looked exactly like an Edwardian out-of-work actor – the effect was spoiled somewhat by his cycle clips. He would park his bicycle against the wall of the porch, remove his cycle clips and glare at us children. Then he would disappear into Teacher's house, bent on mysterious preparations.

We used to get so excited. The performance wasn't very thrilling; the doll was crude and ugly. I was more interested in the ventriloquist's Adam's apple, which bobbed up and down in his throat energetically.

He did the same act every year. One of his standard jokes went as follows:

Doll –	*Glat glis gla glifference glegleen a gliano, a gligar gland glour glace*
Ventriloquist –	*I don't know, what is the difference between a piano, a cigar and my face?*
Doll –	*A gliano glakes glusic, a gligar glakes glou glick, gland glour glace glakes gle glick!*

Hearty laughter and applause followed this witty repartee.

Then one of the boys would collect our pennies and present them to the ventriloquist who hastily shoved them into his pocket, bowed goodbye to the class, mounted his bicycle, with ugly doll strapped on the carrier, and rode away, we supposed, to entertain more schools over the distant horizon. It was a good thing Mother never saw him. He was a poor half-starved looking wretch. No doubt she would have tried to cram a suet pudding down him, as an instant fattener.

Phone : WORCESTER 3386 MALVERN 1080

IF IT'S CARS VANS TRUCKS AND REAL SERVICE

See the MOTOR HOUSE
T. J. DANIEL Ltd.
about it

MAIN FORD & FORDSON DISTRIBUTORS
BATH ROAD, WORCESTER
and MALVERN LINK

MONDAY, JUNE 24th, 1946

Personal Visit of the Popular Villain of Stage, Screen, and Radio Play
TOD SLAUGHTER
and his Company of Famous Players with
JENNY LYNN
In Centenary Performances of the Greatest of Old-time Melodramas—
"SWEENEY TODD"
THE DEMON BARBER OF FLEET STREET
(or "*A String of Pearls*")
Originally Produced at the Britannia Theatre, Hoxton, London, one hundred years ago and played continually ever since

OVERTURE

Characters : *Played by* :

Capt. Mark Ingestre (*of the good ship "Good Hope"*) ... HAROLD BELL
Colonel Blood ... ... ROBERT FORSYTHE
Ben, the Bo'sun (*afterwards Ben the Beadle*) ... BARRY O'NEILL
Pearly Tanner (*a Sailor*) ... VICTOR CRAWFORD
First Sailor ... ... EDWARD STONE
Second Sailor ... ... GEORGE MORRIS
Alderman Jasper Oakley ... FRANK LOGDEN
Eziah (*a Fence*) ... ... WALTER PLINGE
Dr. Lupin (*of the Asylum*) ... STUART LOMAS
Tobias Wragg (*an Orphan*) ... PEGGY CARROLL
Lady Castleborough ... ... ALICIA TRAVERS
Johanna Oakley ... ... ANNE RICHMOND
and
Mrs. Lovatt (*of the Pie-Shop*) JENNY LYNN
Sweeney Todd (*the Demon Barber*) TOD SLAUGHTFR

Synopsis of Scenes :

ACT I
Scene 1—On Board "The Good Hope"
Scene 2—Exterior of Sweeney Todd's Shop
Scene 3—The Interior. (Come Here Tobias!)
4. —Outside the Saloon
Scene 5.—Johanna Oakley's Bedroom

Act II
Scene 1.—Outside the Barber's Shop
Scene 2.—Interior of the Shop. (I'll polish them off)

Act II
Scene 1.—Alderman Oakley's Library
Scene 2.—Underground cellar at Mrs. Lovatt's
Scene 3.—The Library
Scene 4.—Sweeney Todd's Barber Shop

Stage Director ... ... Victor Crawford
Stage Manager ... ... Ed Stone
Booking and Publicity Manager A. J. Neiman
(For TOD SLAUGHTER PRODUCTIONS)

NEXT WEEK
"HI ! THERE"
REVUE

FOR
Service & Repairs to all makes
BATH ROAD GARAGE
J. H. BOWEN F. J. LOXLEY, M.I.M.I.
20, BATH ROAD, WORCESTER
TECALEMIT SERVICE
TECALEMIT
Phone 3500

Showing at the Theatre Royal, Worcester, 1946.

As well as Christmas, Easter and summer holidays, in October we had potato-picking-up holidays. These enabled mothers to do a week's potato picking, and take their children with them to help. Some children also got extended summer holidays to help with hop picking. The summer holidays were the best: they were the longest and we could play outside and watch people that came to buy our vegetables and flowers. We could also help pick sweet peas for the old ladies who came in charabangs from the Black Country. They would park the "Chara" outside and all come swarming out for a sixpenny bunch of flowers. As we picked madly, Mother would bunch them up and tie them with raffia. We called the old gals the "Harriats" – I don't know why. Dad would say: "Here comes a coach of old Harriats." We'd bustle around, putting our flowers on the hedge to catch their eyes. They would buy anything from the country, but they got good value with the cottagers – everything was picked fresh from the garden, and they knew it.

"We 'ad ta cumm out today, ma wench, to miss the rent man," they'd cackle away.

"Hurry up, ladies," the driver of the coach would shout.

"Ooo! Shut your mouth," they'd answer, good-humoredly. They were a jovial bunch. Off the coach went, with the Harriats waving the large sticks of rhubarb Dad had given them as a parting present, the coach full of our flowers and produce.

"See y' next ye-ear," they'd shout.

We liked to see our mother selling a lot of things, because we knew it was the financial supplement for a holiday at the sea. The first holiday at Portsmouth was the most exciting, because as country children, the ships, sailors and the sea were totally alien to us. The second holiday we went on was to Weston-super-Mare, as it was a shorter journey from the Midlands. We didn't like that so well.

Running true to form, I developed six boils on the leg, which were painful and uncomfortable, as I was expected to walk about a lot. Still, I was compensated by being allowed to limp pathetically and wear a large white bandage which passers-by stared admiringly at.

The second trip to Weston was much nicer. We stayed with jolly Mrs Bolton, who understood children. She lived in a lovely house called The Tower which was exactly like a castle with circular rooms; we found this very exciting. Mrs Bolton used to come out with us. We all went to see *Snow White and the Seven Dwarfs* for threepence (1½p) each. This was the first showing of it in this country. We also saw *King Soloman's Mines* with Paul Robeson, for threepence, which delighted us all.

Mrs Bolton told us that Paul Robeson had visited Weston and had been refused admission to the largest and grandest hotel because of his colour. The people of Weston were so infuriated that the management had to make a public apology.

1937 saw the opening of Dudley Zoo and Mrs Wood got up a trip for us to go and see what it was all about. The adults were scandalised and embarrassed at the baboons with their red behinds. We weren't altogether impressed either.

Summer holidays: a memory of riding round the lanes on Sunday morning with Dad on my new old bicycle. We used to go to Mutton Hall to fetch some cabbage plants, or Brant House to get a basket of cherries, passing the millionaire's bungalow on the way. The millionaire was an American, Charles Devine. His bungalow was beautiful, like an old hunting lodge. Mr Devine had had it built as a country retreat.

The locals didn't know for sure that he was a millionaire, they just thought all Americans were. Well, hadn't they all been told so at the pictures? Oh! Mr Devine, where are you now and were you really a millionaire? Come to think of it, I didn't really know for sure what an American was either. When I saw young Charlie Devine flash by in his long- nosed sports car, he looked almost exactly like everyone else. The only difference that I could see, was that he wore his trilby hat perched on the back of his head, whereas the local lads wore their hats tilted over one eye, like George Raft or Bulldog Drummond. It was very puzzling.

In the summertime, we welcomed our friends, the ice cream men, on their "Stop me and Buy one" bikes. Every day they came bumping down the hill to the bridge, looking for customers. Sam, who had thick blonde hair and wore horn-rimmed glasses, rather fancied himself as a lady killer and always made straight for the river side where he'd sit on the lock gate combing his eyebrows, and watched by an admiring crowd of girls. He never seemed to care about ice cream sales, as long as he had a date lined up for that night.

Our special friend was the Eldorado man. He was elderly, with a big white moustache. When we ran out to get an ice cream, he produced a pen knife out of his overall pocket, and methodically cut a wafer in half. We gave him a penny each for our share. He always supplied us with biscuits to go with it – very business-like and polite. All for two pence.

Christmas holidays were pleasant because of Father Christmas and the gifts we received. One Christmas, when I was about five, Auntie Bo took me into Worcester to see Father Christmas at Simes Store (Simes, afterwards Bobbys, now Debenhams). I didn't like Father Christmas: he frightened me. I was more interested in the thing the assistant put the money in. It was screwed into a metal container which whizzed all across the shop, into the office and came back with the receipt and change. It was magic!

Woolworths was known as the "threepence and sixpence store" then. The owners guarantied that nothing cost more than sixpence. In the matter of larger articles, any potential problem was overcome by charging sixpence for a tea pot and threepence for the lid!

Every year, the lady at the nearby castle, kindly treated us school children to the pantomime. We loved *Cinderella* and her song, 'When I Grow Too Old To Dream.' We all wanted to go on the stage when we grew up. We were fascinated by the curtain when it came down in the interval as it had little advertisements stuck all over it: "Visit the Scala Cafe"; "So and So's Dance Studio"; "William Wheatly, Sanitary Engineer". One of our local names, "Albert Farley, Contractor", always brought a cheer.

While staying at Auntie Bo's in the holidays, if it was a wet day, we'd say: "What can we doooooo, Auntie Bo?" She'd fetch out her postcard albums and old photographs of the family. The postcard albums were wonderful –everything a child could wish for. When we had exhausted our interest in these, there were the *Holly Leaves* magazines which were the Christmas editions of *London Illustrated News.* Auntie Bo always had a plentiful supply from years gone by.

On finding pictures of old men and women in bonnets and shawls, doing their Darby and Joan acts, we'd say: 'That's Auntie Bo and Mr Nichols."

"Silly old fools," said Auntie Bo, who had no sentiment for anyone or anything, excepting robins and babies.

The grown-ups had their own style of pleasures. Mother read "novels". She took *Home Companion* every week. The titles of the stories were hilarious: *So You've Left Off Wearing Your Wedding Ring?* was one; *Her Own Dad Turned Her Out* was another. A cover picture told the classic story, a young girl with a white bundle clutched in her wilting arms and dad with fair-isle pullover and pipe, ordering her away from his door, while the snow flakes fell – as expected of them – and anxious mother peered round the net curtain at the window.

I started to read these novels myself and thought they were fascinating. Mum was terribly worried about the effect they would have on my innocent mind. I did find some aspects of them baffling. How could an unmarried woman have a baby, for instance?

Unmarried mums were an endless source of embarrassment to our parents.

Most grown-ups enjoyed going to auction sales in the locality. There were a lot of these and many people furnished their homes in this way. Dad was fond of buying "good clean" feather beds.

Mother would go to a sale near to home, returning later to fetch the wheel barrow, onto which she would load chest of drawers, chairs, tables and once an old spice cupboard. Pictures! There was no end to them. We had nearly as many as the National Gallery! Some of them were pretty, others were pretty awful. We had *Wellington At Waterloo, The Proposal Accepted, The First Sermon, I'll build Ye A Little Cot, The Vicars' Daughter,* and *You Impudent Hussies.*

We didn't realise, or care, that most of them were copies of famous paintings. They were just there to cover up imperfections on the walls, or useful to take down when we needed something to assemble our jigsaw puzzles on. Being a popular pastime for adults and children, we had pictures of every shape and size to accommodate every shape and size of jigsaw.

Mum had a habit of buying "things" from men at the door, if Dad was not around to stop her. She got hold of a job-lot of oil paintings for half a crown once. One of these, *Mountain Sheep,* by C. Jones, in a gilt frame, is still going strong!

Sometimes on Saturdays, she'd go to market and come home with a real bargain. The old wicker chair, which creaked its way through our childhood, was bought brand new, at five shillings, eleven pence (30p)! Mother could also buy a complete bunch of bananas for only one shilling (5p). Jumble sales were another little gold mine, although we took them for granted then. Silver Apostle tea spoons could be bought for a penny each, and once we found a silver coffee pot for sixpence.

CHAPTER 13

DENTISTS, CLOTHES AND THINGS

Toothache was a common occurrence in children. The visit of the school dentist to the Parish Hall, and the opportunity of free treatment, only came round once a year, so if a child had bad teeth, it was usually just a case of putting up with them. Of course, there was always the old-fashioned cure for toothache: putting a spider in a walnut shell and wearing it on a cord around the neck; but by the Thirties we had just about outgrown that one.

I suppose the reasons for our bad teeth were unsuitable and unnutritious food, and lack of cleaning. Though adverts, with laughing, simpering females and dandy *Bryl-creamed* young men, continually beamed out –

Did you Maclean your teeth today?
Ah! I see you did.

or –

She always gets a seat alright,
Because her teeth are Eucryl bright!

– their messages had little effect on most of us. In fact, the only thing that did have effect was our Auntie Nellie making us feel guilty with tales of the gleaming dental perfection of her charges!

Raging toothache often prevailed in the infant room. Our old teacher's remedy was to lay her woolly scarf (which she wore winter and summer) on the desk, and the screaming infant's head would be placed upon it; after a while the screaming would subside to muffled snuffling and usually the child would fall asleep, with the warmth of Teachers' scarf to comfort it.

I was four years old when I paid my first visit to the dentist. The fine autumn morning boded well and, with great excitement, I was dressed in my best hand-knitted, shell-patterned, scalloped-edged, salmon pink dress. It continued excitingly with a hurdy gurdy man playing outside in the road, turning his handle round and round and my being allowed to run out and give him a penny. The walk to catch the bus into town, too, went well . . . but, dear me, what bewilderment, chaos and pain awaited me at the dentist's. Altogether, I had to have four back teeth extracted over two visits. I thought my world had come to an end! Mother bought me a white plaster duck and we had a dish of ice cream in a cafe, but it was little consolation. I was terrified. Dentists nowadays are nothing like those of my youth. There were no red-haired glamour girls, or handsome young men with the charm of Val Doonican and hearts of solid gold. No fear! Dentists in the Thirties were bald-headed, red-nosed, terribly ugly and terribly, terribly cruel. They hated children and were not averse to giving them the occasional slap. I used to imagine that they had all been trained in special schools where they were taught to hate and bully children.

Our dentist lived in a posh house, with a posh waiting room smelling of beeswax and furniture polish. There were oil paintings and samplers on the walls and antique chairs with slender legs which looked like they would break at the teeniest, weeniest kick from the weakest and most unassuming boy on earth. The floor, so highly polished that it positively invited a poor helpless child to slip up and hurt itself, only added to the agony a visit to the dentist could inflict (and I speak from personal memory, having once landed with a terrific crash while tip-toeing gently across the room, to innocently fetch a *Punch* magazine to read; my carelessness bringing instant frowns of alarm from the receptionist).

The receptionist's function was to open the door and escort us reverently into her "Master's" presence. She was middle-aged, bespectacled, with brogue shoes, a jumper suit and pearls. None of "yer white coated blondes with jangling charm bracelets". She would smile politely, but was silent at all times.

We children hated our dentist. I was eight years old before I next paid a visit, and this was only under great pressure and with much fear and general foreboding. My sister and I, together with our friend Edna (a fellow sufferer), held muttered conclaves regarding the punishment we would mete out to him if ever given the chance. It was one of our favourite games on wet days – "How to punish our dentist"; it took precedence over draughts and snakes and ladders, I can tell you! We would grind his teeth to the roots with the drill, and we would drill off both his ears and make a hole in the top of his bald head, ignoring his pleading and screams of pain.

Mother was baffled. She liked the man, thought him a "perfect gentleman" and refused to recognise the monster we conjured up in our imaginations. She said he was a wonderful dentist. He probably was, but we couldn't see it. He took one of her teeth out from time to time. Mother was a bleeder (and I mean that literally!) and felt quite safe in trusting her gums to his tender care. Having had bad experiences with other dentists, she always had to have her gums plugged. Our dentist once told her that the stuff he was plugging her tooth with came from a snake – that was the only thing about him that we found interesting, though we did feel sorry for the snake.

HOURS
9 A.M. TO 8.30 P.M.
THURSDAYS
9 A.M. TO 1 P.M.
UNLESS APPOINTMENT
MADE FOR LATER
HOUR.

60, Lansdowne Street,
Worcester.

James D. McEwan,

Dental Specialist.

[illegible] 1st July 192[illegible]

~~Mr~~ [illegible]

[illegible]

To Professional Services.

£ 1 : 5 :

[illegible]

All Dentures, etc., kept in repair free of charge during the first twelve months after fitting, providing breakages are not caused by careless usage.

My father had all his teeth extracted after the First War. He went to Mr McEwan in Worcester and had gas. While under the influence of the gas, he went berserk and fought Mr McEwan, getting him down on the floor in an attempt to strangle him. Mr McEwan had a wooden leg and had to shout for help, as he couldn't throw Dad off!! How we envied Dad this experience. We kids would have loved to have had a go at our dentist, banging his bald head on the floor and pulling at his red nose. Lovely!

I always thought that our dentist rather fancied Mother. She was what the locals would call a "good looking 'ooman". He certainly gazed admiringly at her, and sent her large numbers of bills. I feel sure he also thought she was a woman of means as she wore good, expensive-looking clothes, most of which Auntie Nellie had sent her. I remember one lovely coat: a sort of brown velour, with a large fur collar. We didn't know what the fur was, but it looked like brown bear: we called it her bear skin. One day, Mother and I were walking up our very steep hill, Mother wearing her bearskin coat, when we overtook the ice cream man who was trying to push his "Stop me and Buy one". He was such a tiny little weak man, and was having difficulties manipulating this heavy vehicle. He asked Mother if she would help him and she reluctantly had to tell him no, as she was recovering from an appendicitis operation at the time. She felt terribly guilty; but fancy asking her to push a "Stop me and Buy one" when she was wearing her exclusive coat! What a cheek! I think that lovely coat finished up on the back of poor Mrs Hollins, round the lane, who had eleven children, no money, not much food, no furniture and a drunken husband.

Mother also had a nice mustard and brown dress and long matching coat, which Auntie Nellie bought for her in a sale at Harrods. It had a look and feel of the jungle about it: we called it her tiger skin. Another interesting garment Mum had, was a suit of brown and white wool, identical to one that Princess Marina

(Duchess of Kent) wore on her honeymoon. It came off the same roll of cloth and was supposed to be exclusive to Princess Marina. We saw a picture of her in *The Tatler* sitting on a wall with the Duke, wearing the self-same styled suit. We were proud of Mum! She didn't often wear it though; she said it wasn't a good fit, but I think she felt secretly guilty, and that she might end up in the Tower, charged with treason.

We had lots of unusual clothes – cast-offs – sent to us. I had a genuine Maclean kilt, which had been passed on through Auntie Nellie's Koebel family (who were related to the Macleans), and thence to me. My kilt was much admired by Gypsy ladies who came to the door selling pegs and laces. They loved tartans and plaids. They also admired my dark hair and looks. I think I secretly hoped that they would kidnap me; I was, and still am, fascinated by the Romany folk. I don't still wish to be kidnapped, but I wish I'd kept that Maclean kilt!

Auntie Nellie used to send large boxes full of cast-off shoes. Most of them were *Daniel Neal's* brown leather school shoes. We children didn't "go" much on them, as they were ugly and clumsy, but the leather was beautiful; when polished it would shine like rich mahogany. Those shoes never wore out and were passed on from us round the village to any children poorer than we were. It was a disconcerting sight to see boys wearing our shoes, sometimes on the wrong feet, and must have been embarrassing for them, too.

We also had boxes of hats, all shapes and sizes. It was great fun trying them on. Panamas and straw hats were the fashion then. Mother used to embroider extraordinary-looking flowers on our hats to cheer them up, and thin chickens that looked as if they had fowl pest. What interesting clothes we received! Shantung silk dresses, pure silk and chiffon scarves, real Fair Isle, scotch wool jumpers. We must have been the finest clad peasants in the district! Dad had a suit of plus-fours once belonging to Colonel Koebel. He wore them for years, very proudly.

Our ruling with regard to clothes was very disciplined and rigid: we had a "best dress" and we had "every day" clothes. Mother used to direct us into what we should wear and lay our clothes out every day, until we were well into our teens. It was therefore very surprising one day when we were at Auntie Bo's playing with a girl from the farm, Rhona Hillier, who was about ten: Auntie Bo asked if she would like to have tea with us; Rhona replied that she would but that she'd have to go home first and change. We went with her and she took us up to her bedroom – a room of her own, mind and opened the wardrobe door. "Which dress shall I put on? *You* choose," she said. We were astonished – she had a rail full of pretty dresses and to think, she had a choice of what to wear!

"Hadn't you better ask your Mother?" we enquired of her, worriedly.

"What for?" she said, looking equally surprised.

Not without envy, we picked out the prettiest dress. It was unusual for a child to have her own room in those days, let alone a whole wardrobe. Thus were the ways of life.

I've strayed far away from the subject of dentists, but would like to add that after much cajoling and pleading with Mother and protesting how cruel ours was, kind-hearted Mother gave in and I was allowed to see the school dentist. The school dentist was a woman and it didn't hurt half so much when she yanked a tooth out. The standard of hygiene, however, left much to be desired. First, we would all stand in a row waiting to sit in the chair, and afterwards, we all stood in a row waiting to spit out, blood running down our chins, from the same chipped enamel mug into the same chipped enamel bowl. The mug and bowl were not washed between child or rinsings.

For all this, I was much happier with the arrangement. Mother wasn't, so it only lasted for one visit. On the way home from school that day, while I was busy spitting away surplus blood in the hedgerow, a chauffeur-driven Daimler, of all things, pulled up, with one of our school governors and his wife inside. Mother accepted a lift from him and off we sailed like royalty. in the leather seats. But in spite of all that, Mother was adament: in future, I must go to my own dentist. I suppose I have to admit that, much as we loathed our dentist, he did a good, if painful job on our teeth; and his yanking out of nerves, draining of abscesses, capping of roots, drilling, grinding, and general boring away saved them from far worse fates. My sister had every tooth in her head stopped (we didn't call them fillings, then). It cost Mother an awful amount of money that she could ill afford, but at least he wasn't like most dentists of his day, union-inclined: one out, all out!

CHAPTER 14

RADIO TIMES

When my sister was five years old, she developed consecutively St Vitus' Dance, an enlarged heart and rheumatic fever; all in all she was ill and disabled for several years. Mother, wishing to compensate her for these troubles and also to help her regain health, wanted to take her to the seaside for a spell; but the doctor said no, she wasn't fit enough to travel. He was probably right, for in those days travelling was a harrowing process involving the changing of many buses and trains, since so few people had cars, and those who did never went as far as the sea; come to think of it, it was doubtful whether some of the local cars would have been any more fit for the journey than my sister!

So, to give her a bit of fun, Mother decided to spend her hard-saved money on a radio – or wireless, as it was always called. This was revolutionary! The only wireless in the district was a crystal set owned by Mr Jeffories at the farm. On Sunday nights after church, he used to put his ear-phones on, and listen spellbound to Albert Sandler playing the violin. "He sounds like a bloomin' bird," he'd say.

But how to go about buying a radio? In those days, it wasn't the simple process of going to an electrical shop or Woolworths, bringing a "tranny" home in your pocket, standing it on the sink unit and tuning it in to Jimmy Young. Oh no! The old wirelesses were clumsy and involving. A lot of wood, a lot of wires (why wireless?), a lot of batteries and an awful lot of patience. To make them go at all, you needed a high tension battery, a low tension battery, a wet battery, an accumulator, an earth wire that was buried in the ground to act as a lightning conductor, a high aerial, and some strong men to put up the pole to hold the aerial.

The first thing to do was for my father to hold a meeting with Mr Davies in the pub. Mr Davies was a bit of a pocket genius. He was a good amateur photographer, an electrician and a wizard with wires – he had built his own radio. Dad asked him if he could make one for us and he agreed. The finished product was a cabinet standing on four spiral legs, quite large: as Dad was fond of saying – "a nice bit of furniture!" When polished up with ornaments, the tea caddy, a vase of flowers and the biscuit tin, it was the highlight of the room.

It was a thing to be proud of, and certainly caused a lot of excitement; even the neighbours came round to stare and wonder at the magic of it.

On the day of the installation, up rode Mr Davies on his bicycle, with friend Griffo pushing the wireless on a truck and Dad standing impatiently by the gate, a large pole for the aerial lying in readiness. Introductions to Griffo, a drop of homemade wine and they were off, heaving the pole and aerial into place. Griffo was all of eighteen stone, Mr Davies, a little man, and Dad, medium to lean in stature. Under such inconsistent weights, chaos prevailed as the pole slipped and sagged all over the place.

At last it was up. Then it was time for Mr Davies to put his technical skill into operation – getting the wireless going and tuning it in properly. The big black knob was turned this way and that, the little brown knob was twisted and pushed, until eventually life appeared. Strange screaming sounds pierced our eardrums. "Oscillating," Mr Davies explained. ("Oscillating," repeated

Mother, proudly, for years to come.)

We were off on our "Radio Times"!

At this time we were into the dance band era. My sister became enamoured with Jack Payne. She wrote to him, and asked him to sing 'See The Little Firemen'. He sent her back a letter and a photograph of the band and said he hoped she'd soon feel better. I, a feeble-four-year old, preferred Ambrose, only because I thought what a lovely red nose he had in my cigarette card picture. My sister also loved Carroll Gibbons and the Savoy Hotel Orpheous. But what a funny name for a man – Carroll!

Children's Hour was the highlight of the day, with Uncle Mac, Auntie Dorothy and Percy Edgar. We used to send silver paper to Uncle Mac for his hospital appeal. On consulting our cigarette cards (the oracle of our youth), we found that Uncle Mac had lost an eye in the war. Wherever was it, my four-year-old brain pondered? Did he stop to look for it before coming home from the war? We also learnt that Uncle Mac had been left for dead on the battlefield. That sounded *very* exciting.

Toy Town was a big favourite, with Mr Growser, Ernest the policeman, the Mayor and Larry the Lamb, played by Uncle Mac.

On our birthdays, both my sister and me had our names read out – at least, we thought we did, not quite catching the words. On another occasion we listened with awe to the tenor voice of Cuthbert Ford singing:

I'm happy as happy can be
I'm having an egg for tea!

We were thrilled! Cuthbert Ford's brother lived in our village! When Dad heard Cuthbert Ford's rendering, however, he growled: "Silly bugger. Ought to be in an asylum." As the years went by, he warmed to this theme of madmen on the radio, and, glancing eagerly around to see if we were interested, would say: "They all come out of a lunatic asylum; they let them out for the programme and lock them up again afterwards."

Into Dad's exclusive society of lunatics went Leonard Henry, Jimmy James, Gillie Potter, Arthur Askey and Richard Murdock; in fact, anyone who could sing "silly" songs, with the possible exception of Leslie Sarony, who wrote and sang 'The Old Sow'. Since this latter was connected with the country and the farm, it was "O.K." by my dad's standards.

Later on, when war started, Tommy Handley became Dad's chief tormentor. On cold winter nights, he'd have to sit through *Itma* in grim desperation, while we females screamed and rolled about with laughter, Finally he'd be driven out to take Paddy the dog for a walk. Anything – anything, to escape from Tommy Handley's insane banter, he said.

Saturday night was bath night. While Mr Davies and Dad supped homemade wine in the pantry, we had tin baths by the fire, sausages for supper and *Music Hall*. On alternative Saturday nights, we had baths, sausages and *Palace of Varieties*. During this, we'd listen to Clapham and Dwyer, Collinson and Breen, Robb Wilton, Norman Long (all teeth and trousers), Albert Wheelan (a song, a smile and a piano), Billy Bennett (almost a gentleman), singer Adelaide Hall, Irish Cavan O'Connor and sometimes Mr Jefforie's "bloomin' bird" Albert Sandler.

There was nothing we didn't listen to – Nosmo King and Hubert, Gert and Daisy, the Kentucky Minstrels, Olive Groves (Classical soprano), Heddle Nash (whom we all called Nettle Rash), and the first disc jockey, Christopher Stone.

Our parents were avid followers of the news broadcasts: Amy Johnson's flights; the kidnapping of the Lindberg baby and consequent arrest of Bruno Hauptman for his killing; the murder of a little girl Mona Tilsley, and Doctor Buck Ruxton's brutal, savage murder of his wife. Mother tried to stop us from hearing these sordid things, but like most mothers, was unsuccessful.

Stuart Hibbard, Chief Announcer, had such a timid voice. One day he made a little "faux pas" and announced: "Now we have Victor Silvestor and his BATHROOM orchestra."

A lot of folk may think that commercial television was a new experience to England at the time. No fear! We had commercial radio in the Thirties –Radio Luxemburg. In the afternoon they used to lay on "soap" operas. *Mary Noble – Back Stage Wife* was one soppy creation that we drooled over for months.

We also had *The Ovaltinies* and *The Cococubs*. Somebody called Jonathan used to introduce *The Cococubs*. I thought he was glorious and cherished secret dreams about him.

One of the radio jingles used to be:

D'y ken John Peel
He enjoys every meal
For pangs of indigestion
He'll never, never feel.
He can eat roast beef
And digest it with zeal
Cause he takes Bisurated Magnesia.

There was also –

High o'er the fence
Leaps Sunny Jim,
Force is the fool
That raises him!

(Sunny Jim being the one our afore-mentioned doll was named after.)

and –

Take Carter's Little Liver Pills
Don't stop, help your ills
Get out of bed
Be happy and so -
Make yourself a nice person to know
Healthy folk are happy folk
They sing, they laugh, they joke
So if you don't feel good
I'll bet you that you would
If you took Carter's Little Liver Pills!

(we enjoyed these.)

On Sunday mornings, Big-Bill-Campbell and his Rocky Mountain Rhythm thrilled me through and through. Those old "cowboy" songs were smashing. Buck Douglas sang 'The Little Red Caboose Behind The Train', 'When The Bloom Is On The Sage' and 'I Bought A Rock For A Rocky Mountain Girl'. Even Dad liked to hear Big-Bill's programme, it was one of our all-time favourites.

We didn't think much of Bing Crosby in the beginning, though. Auntie Bo said crooners weren't quite respectable. It wasn't until the wartime, that we fully appreciated Bing.

What a lot of "comic" songs were thrown at us via our wireless! We weren't allowed to fret about the "doings" of the Nazis in Europe; we were consistently kept cheerful with such songs as –

Today I feel so happy, so happy, so happy,
I don't know why I'm happy,
I only know I am!

Singers Sam Browne and Elsie Carlisle sang 'No – No, A Thousand Times, No!' and 'The Man On The Flying Trapeze.' There was also 'With Her Head Tucked Underneath Her Arm', and 'The Pig Got Up And Slowly Walked Away'. Every Sunday in *The News of the World,* one of these songs was published. I cut them all out and made them into a book and we'd play them on the old harmonium and sing with gusto. Those we weren't familiar with, we made up our own tunes to fit. It was a horrible noise and a stunning shock when we heard the correct tune. Even now, I occasionally sing my homemade version when no one is listening.

Leslie Sarony's 'Ain't It Grand To Be Bloomin' Well Dead!' was a great hit with the public, but was banned, by the B.B.C. and Auntie Bo. She did buy it, but we children were not allowed to listen to it and it was never played on Sunday.

As crooners grew to be more respected, Bert Marlon wailed sadly: 'Here Comes The Bride' and Al Bowley enchanted all female hearts. To borrow a modern expression, we were all "with it". "Each lebe deech," (Ich Liebe Dich), we said with Richard Tauber.

Radio was a great education, and many classic works of literature were serialised: *Lorna Doone, The Mill on the Floss, Castles of England;* Dorothy Summers told her *Epamanandous* stories; and we heard Richard Goollden, in his early days, as Moley in *Toad of Toad Hall.* Goollden used to play a lot of radio parts. He was always the little man – the underdog. We loved him. Hugh Morton was another of our favourite actors, but he played the glorious hero.

Every week, Commander Stephen King-Hall talked to us for ten minutes about interesting things. Mother said he was a real gentleman. One day he talked about Mussolini, saying he was a fascinating character with a strange habit of rolling his eye balls until they completely disappeared, leaving only the whites showing. We practised for hours to try and do this. I'll bet many a child suffered from peculiar eye-maladies after that talk!

At the end of each broadcast, Commander King-Hall would say: "Well, be good, but not *so* good that someone at once says to you: 'Now, what mischief have you been up to?'"

And finally, there was Mabel and Denis Constandourus who gave us endless entertainment with their Grandma Buggins sketches. We were so amused we bought quite a lot of their records, with sketches of *Christmas with the Buggins*, etc.

It was good clean humour and very, very funny.

CHAPTER 15

ANIMALS

This is a book about country doings and country doings always embrace animals. My animals are not going to be like James Herriot's, or even Fred Archer's, and they are certainly not like Gerald Durrell's. My animals are off-beat. I'll start with the humble flea.

What has happened to the flea
Well known for his energy?

This is a poem I started to write and didn't complete, but it sums up the situation. When we moved into our cottage, the walls were covered in fleas. How and why we didn't know. There were no insect sprays or D.D.T. powders in those days, only *Jeyes* fluid powder and carbolic soap. So my mother rubbed and scrubbed and hoped for the best.

They frequently got into our beds. When Mother was shaking up the feathers, she'd go: "Waitaminute, waitaminute, waitaminute – got it!" and another flea would bite the dust. The knack was to catch them between fingers and crack them with the thumb nail. Poor little blighters – we didn't mind them so much that they deserved that fate! But it is true that many people did get plastered in flea bites. So that leaves me nothing but to repeat – "What has happened to the flea, well known for his energy?"

Living slap bang in the middle of the country side, one might think that people were used to cows and bulls. Not a bit of it. I have always been a *bit* frightened of cows and I never saw the sight of a bull until I was over twenty. They certainly didn't stand around in fields waiting for some unsuspecting, red-dressed female to scramble over the stile, as we were led to believe from the *Just William* books, comics and such like.

The only bull I had any knowledge of as a child, was the one at the farm down the road from our cottage. He was supposed to be kept in the old barn adjoining the house and occasionally, when the wind was in the right direction, a terrible pong would waft upwards. "Farmer Briggs' bull 'as turned over again," people would say with a laugh. I never saw this bull and don't know if it really existed.

Hunt meets were common. During the hunting season, on their six mile walk from Fernhill Heath Kennels, the foxhounds, the huntsmen and the horses would pass our house, and on their return, the huntsmen would stop at our gate for a glass of homemade wine. Mother would take them out a tray of glasses and pass the wine round, trying to ignore the horses that nuzzled her. The Chief Whip rewarded her one day with a fox's brush, which she cured in methylated spirits.

Mother was terrified of horses. It was the one big fear of her life. At the same time she felt tremendous compassion for them. Many a time, I saw her follow a horse and cart up the steep hill by our cottage, to ensure that the man was not beating the horse to hurry him up. She could not stand the thought of any cruelty and I can see her now, in her pinafore, following behind a Gypsy wagon to see fair play. It worried her to see the lurcher dogs tied at the back of the wagons and the small sturdy ponies pulling their hearts out. Many a large farmer she took on verbally, aggrieved at his treatment of animals. One such occasion, she followed after a suspicious-looking travelling man, whose poor horse was labouring frantically to pull a wagon up the hill. When they reached the brow of the hill – the steepest point – her suspicions were justified. The wretched man was putting straw under the horse's belly and preparing to set fire to it, thus forcing the frightened horse to move. Mother really let fly and the shame-faced man stopped his unspeakable doings. She then hurried back down the hill to the nearest house with a phone and got the local policeman, who came pedalling furiously along on his bicycle and set off in pursuit of the man and his horse. He caught up with him at the next cross-roads and gave him a real dressing-down, threatening him with prosecution, prison, or the cat-o-nine-tails. Those were the days. People took notice of police threats!

On the subject of horses, the death of any horse was a sad event. They led a hard and harrowing life on the farms, but many were well-loved and the thought of a glorious old chestnut, black or dappled mountain of flesh quivering to an eternal halt, is sad to contemplate. But for me, there was always a certain excitement in the event as well; this was because of the dead-horse-man – that was what we called him. He was a little bowler-hatted man in a raincoat and leggings, and he'd come trotting by in his horse and trap to pick up any dead carcases from the farms. Playing in the road, we'd hear the familiar trit-trot, coming round the corner. Mother would dash out and hustle us into the house until he'd passed by, then she would stand by the window saying: "Poor thing, poor thing." We'd rush back out into the road in time to see the dead-horse-man starting the climb up the hill, with the horse lying across the back of the trap covered in an old blanket, its poor dead hoofs and legs jolting up and down as they went. It was sad, of course, but we felt the fascination of death as most children do.

I must mention also the stallions that came periodically round the farms to visit the mares. These were huge, dangerous-looking creatures, with great legs and flowing manes. A man would hang on to their heads, as they came, eyes rolling, slipping and slithering down the hill. The man in charge always seemed to be small and never looked strong enough to control them. My greatest fear (and that of my mother's) was to meet one of them as they walked the roads. I have no doubt that they were as dangerous as they looked and I can't imagine them walking the traffic roads today.

Near Grandad's cottage on the court estate, lived a mule named Johnny. He was a left-over from the war where he had been out in the trenches, pulling gun carriages and trucks for the army. After the war he was bought up by our local lord, or 'Lordy' as we called him, and came to work on the farm.

He was a temperamental animal; little wonder I would say, after the life he had led. Some days he wouldn't work at all; when the harness and collar was put on him, he refused to budge. It made no difference if the waggoner lashed him with the whip. He wouldn't move. Since the old lord had given instructions that he was not to be forced, the men would let him go and he'd canter up past Grandad's cottage, sweating and steaming and rolling his eyes. As he came, we could hear his hoof beats and harness jangling, and we'd get out of the way mighty quickly! Life was full of fears to us kids then! The old mule would go straight through the open gate, into his stable and stay there until his temper had passed, maybe a day or two later. Then he would be ready for work again.

A lot of people kept a pig in the garden sty, so this involved a yearly visit from the pig-killer. That was a horrible gory business. I'm sure a lot of folk became attached to their pig and "killing" day was looked forward to with mixed feelings. Pig-killers had various reputations for humanitarian devices or otherwise. Our local pig-killer rejoiced in the unlikely, innocent name of Maiden. When the great day came round, it was a question of: "Oh, maiden, my maiden, where are you?"

Everything would be ready and awaiting his services: pots, pans, buckets, tables scrubbed, and boiling water bubbling away. Not until two thirty however, when the pubs had closed, would he put in an appearance; by this time he was always half-cut, which was more than could be said for the pig! Maybe he nurtured tender feelings his profession belied, and felt he couldn't get by without this "Dutch" courage.

In the animal world, as in every thing else, we were enmeshed in fancies. "If you keep picking a kitten up, it won't grow!" folks would say. "Pick a guinea-pig up by the tail and its eyes will drop out", "Never allow a dog to stare in the fire, or he will go blind". I could see some logic in this latter saying, but we had a dog who stared continually into the fire, each and every winter evening, and he never lost his sight. The fire must have held some fearful fascination for him; if a bit of ash or coal plummetted down into the ash-pan, he would leap up and rush under the table, keeping up surveillance from there. I guess he had been burned with a hot spark sometime in his life.

He was about four years old when we adopted him. His name was Paddy and he was a cross-bred Sealyham, a great little dog, very intelligent. When the peas were ready to pick in the garden, he would trot up and down the rows, picking his own and shelling and eating them. He knew the exact time that they were ready to pick, even before my father did!

Paddy was also a hero in his own right and should have been awarded the Dickon medal for bravery. When living with his former owner, he was out playing in a nearby field with the dog from next-door, whose name was Trigger. Someone, probably out rabbiting, fired a shot and the bullet hit Trigger in the back, rendering him paralysed in the legs. Paddy ran off home and yelped continually at the neighbour's door. As soon as she opened it, he seized her apron in his mouth and pulled and pulled and nudged her, until she followed him to where Trigger lay – thus saving Trigger's life, who subsequently recovered and lived to be a good old age. The vet and the neighbour were full of praise and admiration for Paddy. He was a great little character. Another cute trick that he had, was to beg for the "Harriats". He would wait by the gate when coaches went by, then sit up on his haunches as the old girls approached. They loved him and used to give him sweets and biscuits. He was so crafty. As he got older, he would sit up for so long that he'd drop off to sleep, quite oblivious of what he was doing. Very amusing, but his greed did tend to make his waist-line rather rotund. He eventually died from distemper at the age of twelve. We were ignorant then of doggy complaints and thought he just had a bad cough. By the time the vet came he was too ill to save; it was only good care and Paddy's stamina that had kept him going for so long.

Animals, like people, had never heard of hypochondria as such then. If dogs looked off-colour they were just given *Bob Martin's Condition Powers* – and liked it! It was only in extreme cases that we would have considered consulting a vet.

Apart from Paddy and the fleas, the only other domestic creatures we had were hens. Well, what can you write about a hen? Betty MacDonald might have got a whole book out of them, but there is precious little *I* can find to say! Apart from pecking, fluttering, stalking and laying, they didn't do much. I suppose it was nice to have fresh eggs from time to time, but all hens were run-about, then. The cursed battery system had not been invented. Hens walked freely, calves followed their mothers around lush meadows and pigs rooted and grunted in orchards.

Happy days!

EXPLANATIONS – CONTINUED

"Well, Mother," says my daughter – she always calls me Mother when she is exasperated – "that may be, but we live in a different sort of world today: a technical, mechanical age."

She spits on a dock-leaf and rubs it on her nettle-sting.

"Do we?" I say.

PART TWO

STRANGERS ON THE BAR.

When my mother poked the fire on winter days, and if she saw a little bit of smut on the bar of the grate, she'd say: "There's a stranger on the bar." That meant we would have an unexpected visitor.

With the coming of the war, we were to receive many strangers, who quickly became friends: Scots, Irish, Welsh, Americans, Poles, Czechs, Italians and the occasional odd German. Even the people from adjacent villages became friends and that was unusual, to say the least.

This book is mostly about our strangers on the bar.

CHAPTER 1

WINTER AND A BIT OF WAR

On January 1st, 1940, we awakened to the sound of loud crashing and banging; Dad was shouting up the stairs to us to get up quickly and come and see the river: it was frozen over. The river wasn't the only thing that was frozen! and it was with great reluctance that my sister and I crawled out of the warm nests we had made in our feather beds, into the icy cold atmosphere of our bedroom.

We hastily donned every vestige of clothing we could find, then crept shivering downstairs to drink a hot cup of tea by the fire, while Dad paced impatiently up and down, chivvying us to hurry and see this strange phenomena. We put on our coats, pixie-hoods and mittens, not stopping to wash even our faces: Mother said we might get frostbite, going out into the cold after being by the warm fire.

Off we set, down the icy road and round the corner to the bridge, resenting every crunchy step we took. Dad walked yards ahead, shouting back to us to hurry up before the ice melted. He needn't have worried! The river was frozen into solid blocks of ice, two – three feet square. The ice blocks were crashing away down the river, taking everything before them. The landing stages had already gone and Mr Stocker's motor-boat, in which he took summer visitors for sixpence rides up and down the river, lay battered, keeled over and stern uppermost. We stared in amazement. We had never seen anything like it. However, we were not so amazed as to forget our own frozen bodies; as soon as we could, we got out of Dad's clutches and made for home and the warm fire.

When the milkman arrived, Dad hurried out to inject some of his enthusiasm. Our milkman was a young absent-minded farmer, always in a tearing hurry. "He'll meet himself coming back one day," Dad used to say. He certainly had to slow down that morning. Dad sent him off with a flea in his ear, to look at the river. "Probably forget what he's gone to look at," said Dad.

We were in the middle of a bitterly cold winter. On Boxing Day the ice was so thick on the telegraph wires, that they broke and sagged down into the road and garden. By the time the day was out, we had entertained a houseful of post office repair men to hot tea, homemade wine, pickles and cheese.

As well as those extreme weather conditions, we also had to put up with the war; not that that affected us much in the beginning of 1940. Neville Chamberlain, the man with the umbrella, had taken us through the "Peace in our Time" bit; we all had umbrellas for Christmas presents and carried them proudly.

"He saved our country," said Dad.

"I remember his father Joseph," said Auntie Bo, proudly.

Nosmo King, who was really Vernon Watson, came on Saturday night's *Music Hall* and recited a monologue about, "The man who used his common sense". He was applauded to the rafters! We listened with tears in our eyes. Suddenly Hitler's antics came to full force in Austria and Poland. Nobody liked Chamberlain any more.

"Never could trust the bl . . . Chamberlains," said Dad.

"I remember his father Joseph," said Auntie Bo, sadly.

The Sunday that war was declared, September 3rd, was a lovely hot summer's day. Visitors strolled along the river side, everything was peaceful. We waited for something traumatic to happen – it didn't. People said: "It'll be over by Christmas."

"That's what they said in 1914," said Dad, darkly.

"I'm glad I never had any sons," Mother said.

Mr Pearson, who had always behaved somewhat like a hermit with his scruffy clothes and a black patch over one eye – very frightening to us children in the 1930s – suddenly emerged as our benign air raid warden. He came bustling along one autumn to fit us for our gas-masks, wearing a clean raincoat, a clean face and no patch. It was amazing! How proud we were when we collected the masks from the Parish Hall. We carried them everywhere. We even took them to the outside lavatory – they stood by us on the wooden bench seat, a comforting sight, there to protect us should the Germans drop gas bombs as we sat there in our vulnerable position. I took mine to school, tied with string around my back like a satchel. The gas-masks were in little cardboard boxes. My sister, who had recently started work in Woolworths (and could therefore afford it), bought a *real* crocodile-skin bag for sixpence to carry hers in. I was green with envy. We carried them and carried them and carried them. Then we gradually forgot them.

Mr Pearson, so dedicated a warden at the start, walking by our houses at night shouting: "Put that light out!" if a chink showed through our blackout curtains, seemed to grow disenchanted and finally retreated back behind the shelter of his black patch.

What a laugh we got out of our gas-masks! There were inevitable jokes about smells and the blackout and when the men emptied the lavatory buckets we'd say: "Put your gas mask on," and other ribald comments.

Things didn't alter much at school: we had to write on the front and back covers of our exercise books to save paper; a sprinkle of evacuees from Birmingham arrived: and our school windows were pasted over with strips of paper to prevent glass flying should there be an air raid, but that was about all.

Three bombs were dropped in the area during the whole of the war. One fell in a meadow along the river banks and caused no damage; one fell in a field by a row of council houses; and the other landed in the same spot quite a time later, which was pure coincidence. On both these latter occasions, the roofs were blown off the houses, but there were no casualties. Our postman Len lived in the one house. He was inflamed! What he wasn't going to do to that bugger of a Hitler was nobody's business. Every time he came to empty the post-box he ranted and raved as though Hitler were conducting a personal vendetta against him. We secretly thought it was rather amusing.

With the coming of war, we had a new set of villains to identify with.

When my mother was a child in 1900, living in Upton Snodsbury, the village folk disciplined their children by saying: "If you're out after dark the Mormons 'ull get you," (or Jack the Ripper, as the case might be).

In the Thirties, the Brummies who moved to the country said to their kids: "Get out of the 'orse road, or the Bobbie 'ull 'ave yu."

We locals weren't intimidated by the police. They were all friends to us. Half of their duty hours were spent in our scullery drinking Dad's wine.

So now we had new baddies to utilize – the Nazis. "You're just like that Hitler," I said to my arch-enemy, Stanley, – who was doing quite a passable imitation of Charles Laughton in *The Hunchback of Notre Dame.*

Any fat person we likened to "that Goering bloke", and to any one who told lies we said: "You're just like that Goebells." – we pronounced it Go-bells. With my eye brows, I thought I looked like Rudolph Hess, but no one noticed, thank goodness, so I kept it a close secret.

"Blooming old Hitler," we chanted in the playground.

"Be quiet," shouted Teacher.

"Ooo, Teacher's a spy," we said. We didn't imagine for a minute it was our manners and grammar she was after. We went home and told our parents: "Teacher's a spy."

"Don't be silly" they said. End of that episode!

On the wireless and in the papers, we were told to economise and save all we could to help "The War Effort". The men on army reserve had already been called up and a few young locals joined. They went proudly off, telling us that they'd soon settle old Hitler's' hash.

We were so good-humoured about the Germans. We couldn't believe they were as bad as all that – just a bunch of cads, really.

"You wait," said my dad, soaking his feet in strong washing soda to save the soap. "You wait 'till they start, you'll know something about it then. The only good German's a dead one" etc. When they did start and we awoke to realisation, we were livid.

"What did I tell you?" said Dad triumphantly, rubbing his soaking feet until they squeaked and made our fillings jump to attention. He carried on as though it was our fault, personally.

From that cold winter we emerged into the crisis of the attempted invasion and the evacuation from Dunkirk. Suddenly "We're going to hang out the washing on the Ziegfreed line", didn't quite fit into the plan of things any more. We were puzzled.

War dragged on into the summer. Still nothing much happened in our little world. We wrote to soldiers and sailors overseas. They wrote back and told us not to worry, they were taking care of things. We *were* grateful. We continued to joke about Hitler and Mussolini, who had by that time joined forces with Hitler.

We sang:

Whistle while you work,
Mussolini bought a shirt,
Hitler wore it, Churchill tore it,
Whistle while you work.

Being so disillusioned with Chamberlain we welcomed Churchill, so strong and dogged, who was taking over – although he had yet to prove himself.

"Look at the mistakes he made over the Dardinelles," said Dad, dubious as ever.

It seems strange now, with all the information that is known and recorded about the Second World War, that at the time we in the country didn't take much notice of the bombing in the cities. Of course, we heard reports on the wireless and people arrived from Birmingham, haggard and drawn with the worry of it all, many having lost their homes and possessions; but generally, we were pretty unaware of things. Perhaps we would have been more aware if we'd had television then, a visual guide being so much more compelling.

Sometimes we heard the bombers going over at night and the throb-throb of the Yunkers. One night we saw the sky lit up by terrific fires in the distance, and we mourned the loss of much of the Portsmouth we had remembered from happy holidays.

On the night that Coventry was severely bombed, my sister was sitting on top of a double-decker bus, on her way home from Woolworths. The distant glow in the sky and the noise of the planes was so intense that the driver pulled the bus into a traffic lay-by and turned all the lights out; and there they waited for an hour, the passengers silent, many in tears.

Then some soldiers on the bus started to sing songs like 'Tipperary', 'Pack Up Your Troubles' and 'Land of Hope and Glory'. The passengers slowly joined in, the tension broke and the bus continued on its way.

CHAPTER 2

THE DEVIL YOU KNOW

By the end of the first year of the war, I was reaching my last year at school. Strangely, I had developed an affection for school, even quite liking Teacher and realising that she wasn't the ogre I had thought her to be, but just a rather lonely middle-aged lady.

I was not ailing any more, so I no longer had time away from school. As a result, my marks improved in all subjects except arithmetic, and I was awarded the prize for the best work in the school year – *The Schoolgirls Own Annual,* donated by the local publican's wife. I was pleased to receive the honour, but as I was reading books at home like *Gone with the Wind* and *Les Misérables* this prize was a bit misplaced.

The mainstay of my life at this time, was my old heavy iron bicycle which Dad had bought for ten bob (50p). I longed for a new sports bike, with modern cable brakes and a saddle bag, but this was a far away dream. The old bicycle, named Freddie (although I suppose it was really a lady bike, having no cross-bar) piloted me to school and back, home for dinner and miles around the endless country lanes. Some dinner-times I went to my friend Gladys's home, a mile along the opposite road to ours. Gladys lived on a cosy little farm. The cows looked cosy, the kitchen looked cosy and Gladys' mother, who made us hot strong cocoa and fussed over us, was cosy –

plump with apple cheeks and a bun, just like you would expect a farmer's wife to look. Gladys and I joined The Cococubs and were always making secret signs to one another. Gladys left school before me and, departing into the world of work, she proceeded to grow up.

Christmas came. We had a party at school and I wore my red velvet dress. Mother made me wear a jumper underneath as it wasn't very warm – the sleeves of the jumper showed, the collar stood up around the neck, and somehow the aura of "sophistication" was not quite what I had hoped to achieve.

We took bread and whatever we could scrounge from our mothers, but there wasn't much to spare – paste sandwiches and homemade cake was about all we could stretch to. Food was getting very short.

All in all, we had a good time: we played party games and I was presented with my prize. Teacher took me on one side and asked if I would not reconsider leaving and stay on at school until Easter. I said no, but with some reluctance. All the years I had longed to leave school and be free. Suddenly I wasn't sure, the future seemed uncertain. The idea of going to work was terrifying.

Teacher had tried to persuade Mother to let my sister and me sit for the grammar school scholarship. Our aunties were also keen for us to try. But we rebelled strongly against it. Mother said we were too delicate to travel to school and back every day, especially with the war being on, and Dad said we couldn't have afforded the clothes and books we would need, anyway. So we happily got out of this further education. Oh! how short-sighted the young were then.

Dad was keen for everyone to get to work as quickly as possible, to earn money and help support themselves. It was the way he had been brought up to think; we didn't blame him. Mother never appeared to be bothered at all about money and couldn't care less who went to work and who didn't, as long as they were happy; and that was the way she had been brought up.

So here I was, leaving school. Most children who left school on the Friday had a job lined up to start on the following Monday, usually land work or gardening for the boys, and service for the girls. One day they were children, in socks and old shabby clothes; the next they had become skivvies, with long aprons and dresses nearly to the ground to allow for growth, their frightened little faces peeping out from huge white mob-like caps.

Fortunately, I was spared all that. I loitered at home that winter, like Mr Micawber, waiting to see what would turn up. I took our dog Paddy for long walks and went up to see Grandad and Auntie Bo. I dusted the sideboard and whatnot and peeled the potatoes for Mother, I shopped and paid the rent in the village for Dad. The locals must have thought it a very strange set-up! They weren't used to anyone over the age of fourteen staying at home.

One day, as Easter approached, Mr Seymour, who kept the garage, café and the shop by the bridge, stopped his Morris 8 outside the gate and asked Mother how she would feel about my helping in his shop. Seymour's shop had launched several local girls into the great wide working world. It sold mainly sweets, rock, cigarettes and minerals, with ice-cream and souvenirs and toys for holiday visitors. Mother asked me how I would like to work there. I said fine, or words to that effect, but I was secretly terrified. Mr Seymour was so sophisticated. He wore plus-fours and a matching tweed cap; mowed his lawn and putting coarse, striding up and down manfully, wearing a striped bathing-suit top; while we locals cringed admiringly at the railings.

Everybody respected Mr Seymour's talents. He was always on hand if people were in trouble, and was forever rushing someone to hospital to have impatient babies or emergency ops., or taking pets to the vet. I don't know what most of us would have done in times of trouble without Mr Seymour, *and* his telephone.

But I was terribly frightened of him: he spoke well and used such big words, he was very intimidating to a fourteen-year-old. Dad said he was a clever man: he could also fly an aeroplane, do any type of mechanised and electrical work, and owned a violin.

So it was decided: on Easter Sunday I started work there. All my nervous traits returned. There were lots of people living in the house that I didn't know or understand. Edna from the locks worked in the cafe; I was supposed to work in the shop, but I also washed up and helped her in the cafe, which I hated, being so timid. If anyone condescendingly gave me a sixpence tip, I would blush scarlet and wish that I was dead. I worked from ten am till about seven pm and earned eight shillings (40p) a week. I had two meals daily, lunch and tea, which I was too nervous to eat, but too timid to refuse, so that my mealtimes were spent chewing and chewing large blobs of food that refused to go down my panic-stricken throat. Most of the food found its way into my apron pocket, to be deposited later, a sticky mess, into some unsuspecting hedgerow! I had one half-day holiday a week – Friday (ever since, Friday has always been my favourite day and I think this is the reason). I worked from Easter until September, when the season ended. Once again, my self-assurance had taken a rapid plunge downhill.

On Armistice Day, November 11th, we all went to church. It was cold and damp and my sister caught a cold and cough which quickly turned to pleurisy. She was very ill and it was a great worry to Mother, so Dr Deana, the chest and lung specialist, came out from Worcester to examine her. At the same time, Grandad, who was then eighty-seven and had latterly been growing more frail, became unwell. The doctor said it was just his age and gave Auntie Bo a bottle of medicine – I think to satisfy her, more than to help Grandad who had never taken any medicine or pills in his life; the full content of Auntie Bo's medicine drawer in the kitchen table was a tape of *Aspro* and a tin of bi-carbonate of soda. Grandad, although a frail old man, never seemed to get all the ailments we do today; you never heard him complain of back-ache, headache or bad feet.

He never seemed to catch colds and if his blood-pressure was raised, he wasn't aware of it. His only concession to old age was warm, woolly vests and the two stone and aluminium hot water bottles Auntie Bo put into his bed at night, wrapped in her old stockings to prevent burning his feet.

The last week of his life, Grandad lay in bed, quietly slipping away, in the same peaceful manner that he had lived. It was the pleasantest possible way for old people to die.

Mother was so busy and worried looking after my sister, she could not do much to assist Auntie Bo with the funeral arrangements. As it was felt that she should not be on her own at this time, I was sent to stay with her for a while. She soon poo-pooed this idea!

"Its not right for you to be in the house alone, with your Father lying upstairs, Flo!" said Auntie Laura.

"Nonsense," said Auntie Bo. "He never hurt me when he was alive and he certainly won't now he's dead." She actually laughed. Auntie Laura thought this a very irreverent thing to do! But Auntie Bo was like that, she was unshakeable. She cared little for the sensibilities of man, beast – or sister-in-law!

In the few nights before the burial, while Grandad lay in the back-room upstairs, in the same feather bed he had slept in since he had been widowed in 1916; Auntie Bo and I slept downstairs on the sofas. Auntie Bo was small, so she slept on the upright horse-hair, while I sprawled myself lankily on the old leather sofa, propped up either end by a brick. We kept a big fire going all night – that was probably the only time in her life that Auntie Bo slept in a heated room, she didn't believe in such things. The apple tree branches tapped gently on the window, the door latch rattled. Grandad had died on my birthday, November 20th. I somehow couldn't rid myself of a guilty feeling that his dying had something to do with my birthday. Strange is the imagination.

Christmas came and Auntie Bo put holly behind the pictures;

this was the extent of Christmas decorations in those days: no tinsel, no fairies, no lights, no garlands and chains, just holly and mistletoe. Mrs Evans next door, strongly disapproved and thought it was wrong to decorate thus, while still in mourning for Grandad.

Auntie Bo and me lived very quietly; it was dull for a young girl. There was an old wireless but Auntie Bo only listened to the news. I liked to listen to plays, but she had a disconcerting habit of coming into the room in the middle of a play and switching off the wireless because it was "too noisy", or she wanted "to tell me something". When I protested, she was surprised and said: "Well, you can put it on again later." She could never understand that the wireless didn't work like that. She seemed to think that when you turned it off, it automatically stopped broadcasting! It was too frustrating, so I gave up and turned to books instead. I used to go to bed early with my candle and try to read John Galsworthy's *Forsytes*, but I found them a boring bunch.

At this time, I was going to Confirmation classes at the church every Sunday afternoon. This I found nerve-wracking, one reason being that come Confirmation day, I was to borrow my friend Edna's white dress. We always had special, plain, silky dresses for the occasion, but they were expensive and clothes were rationed, so a lot of dresses were borrowed and lent. The trouble was, Edna was very plump at that time and I was very thin. When I tried the dress on I hated it – it hung over my shoulders and was far too long; but there was no possibility of altering it: it was borrowed; in any case, even it it wasn't, Mother was too busy and harassed to do it and neither myself nor Auntie Bo were any good at sewing. I was condemned to wear it as it was.

Somebody was looking out for me, however, and I was given a last minute reprieve – yellow jaundice! My sister no sooner recovered and Mother was in for another dose with me. For days, the doctor had no idea what the matter was and called constantly. Then he saw my jet black urine and that confirmed it. Poor Mother battled bravely on with my constant vomiting and delirium, trying to convince me that there were no little men climbing up the chimney.

I ate nothing for three weeks, then suddenly felt better and asked for a baked dried potato. That was the start of my recovery. The doctor said I had caught the illness from the rats which ran around the house. I ate no butter, fats or bacon for months afterwards. That was a blessing really, as by then we were rationed and food was in short supply.

The jaundice was horrible and dirty, but at least it meant I could have a reprieve from Auntie Bo's rigid life, and it was a treat to listen to everything on the wireless at home.

Dad's friend, Mr Davies, came most nights. He used to bring me jigsaw puzzles: a magnificent one of an Indian Chief's head with the feathered head-dress and a similar one of a lion's head, both very difficult to do, but fascinating. I got so good at them that I could do *Waiting for the Coach* in twenty minutes flat.

CHAPTER 3

MORE TEENAGERS

There's been a lot written about teenagers in latter years so I propose now to add my two-pennorth.

Teenagers did not exist before the last war; we just had young people who were more or less ignored by adults. Young people change so speedily: one day they're ugly, the next day pretty, one day untidy and uncaring, the next smart.

In the summers when I was thirteen and fourteen, I realized that an aid to beauty could be easily acquired at no cost. It was called the sun. All I had to do was to put an old blanket on the lawn and stretch out in the noon heat. My face soon became pink, then red, and by nightfall I had turned a very pleasing tan. This also disguised my ugly arms by bleaching the hairs, so was an asset all round.

Our neighbour Mrs Passey was worried about these goings-on. Her head would appear over the hedge, remonstrating in horror. "I don't know *how* you can be in that hot sun," she'd say, "I couldn't do it." She would then proceed farther on down the road and stand talking to Mother over the gate, arms folded, for about an hour in the self-same sun. I couldn't quite grasp the logic of this. Mother was also worried. She had been brought up to think that pale skins were gentile and ladies (real ones) always wore hat and gloves for protection. She was also uneasy for fear I should get sunstroke or have a fit. I didn't, but I did acquire a lovely brown skin.

After a while, to appease Mother, I used to smother my face in protective olive-oil, which gave me a foreign appearance and caused passers-by to stare, and gnats and flies to gather eagerly around.

War or no war, we still struggled to appear beautiful. I tried some concoction called *Velute-de-Dixor,* which was a powder cream and very popular with the ladies. For some reason we always thought that powder and cream should only be put on the end of the nose to stop it shining and on the middle of the cheeks. We would never have put make-up round the eyes for fear of going blind, and lip-stick was only applied round the outer-rim of the lips for fear of our being poisoned if we ate it by mistake!

The *Velute-de-Dixor* gave me a smooth skin, the sun-tan disguised my panda-like eyes and hairy arms, and made me look altogether healthier, so gradually I began again to gain some self-confidence. Too much, some would say, and did. "She's too purgy by half," said our doctor. I cheeked, sulked, irritated and flirted like mad. It was wonderful. I also sweated. Boy! how I sweated. My woolly jumpers and cardigans became a thick uncomfortable mat under the arms, and the colour ran in my summer dresses. In the end I brought some rubber dress shields from Woolworths. Clumsy things they were, they had to be sewn underneath the sleeves and were not a success: they protected my dresses, but made me sweat all the more. They were so bulky and caused my arms to be permanently akimbo. On hot days, a strong smell of rubber followed in my wake and friends edged noticeably away with pinched nostrils. I was in despair until my Auntie Nellie said: "Why don't you use a deodorant?" So I bought a small bottle of *Odo-ro-no,* dabbed it under my armpits and lay on the bed, arms raised for half an hour to allow it to dry – that was the draw-back with early deodorants, they took such ages to dry. The effect lasted for three days, according to the bottle, so I didn't wash very often for fear of spoiling the effort.

Nevertheless, that was the end of my worries regarding perspiration but another anxiety for poor Mother, who was convinced I would become desperately ill on account of my sweat glands seizing up.

"Nonsense," Auntie Nell would say. "There are sweat glands all over the body to take care of that." Mother also worried about this time, in case, during puberty, we developed big noses like the noses of her in-laws.

But on the whole, things were definitely improving on the home and beauty front; thanks to my luxurious long hair, *Velute-de-Dixor, Minor's Liquid Make-Up* and a dab of Mothers' stale rouge, I was certainly better looking.

One day Mother's old friend Florrie visited us. She said of me: "She has a perfect oval face." When she'd gone I asked Mother what that meant. "Egg- shaped," she replied to my disappointment.

However, while conditions were favourable on the home and beauty front, elsewhere the war raged on. We were effected by food and clothes rationing and a general shortage of everything, but on the whole, we managed. It was all rather exciting, in fact; it brought out the pioneering spirit in our nature.

Convoys of soldiers started to pass through our hamlet, waving and shouting to us and occasionally stopping to ask the whereabouts of a shop or a pub. We weren't supposed to tell them the name of our village, or how far away they were from towns, or indeed any information that would be of interest or gain to the enemy. We had to treat everyone as a potential spy. It was a bit daft, really. We were rather obsessed by spies. Anyone, even life-time acquaintances, who did anything slightly unusual became a suspect.

One young man, Leslie, whom some of us girls cherished secret romantic thoughts for, was always on the suspect list. For one thing, he was not in the services, neither was he doing any war work, nor was he in the Home Guard or Civil Defence; in fact, he didn't seem to do much at all and was rather scornful about the whole business of the war. He played the piano beautifully in the pubs, so I suppose he was an asset to the jolly sing-songs of wartime. But in this too he was perverse, playing 'The Blue Danube'; 'Liszt's Hungarian Rhapsody' and his own compositions, while the customers grumbled impatiently for 'We'll Meet Again' and 'There'll Always be an England'.

Sometimes he managed to get petrol for his old car which, of course, was strictly rationed. The young local fellows were very suspicious of him, jealous I would think.

One day, a land girl (not a local) had a date to meet him. He turned up wearing a mauve-coloured suit and white socks. She refused to go out with him, and this confirmed everyone's conviction that he was a spy – whoever heard of an Englishman wearing a mauve suit and white socks? Especially in wartime.

We chummy girls, who didn't like the land-girl on principle, said it served her right and anyway, we didn't know *what* he could see in her as she had flared hairy nostrils! That in turn cast *her* in a suspicious light – didn't all spies have hairy nostrils?

There were hardly any cars or lorries around at this time and few delivery vans. All sign posts were taken down, but as there were no holiday-makers or visitors, this didn't matter; the soldiers had their own maps for reference. Sometimes mock battles were staged and pontoon bridges were erected over the river. Soldiers rushed hither and thither trying to look fierce, while we girls stood on the river bank, giggling and making rude remarks.

The soldiers told us to go away; that we couldn't cross the bridge because it had been blown up, and didn't we know there was a war on? All this, of course, caused great hilarity among the villagers. "You'll have to swim for it tonight, lad," they'd shout to the postman, who would reply with some colourful language. But being so patriotic he didn't really mind being a few hours late; after all, it was all the fault of that Hitler and his cronies, and we should be united in putting paid to them. We didn't mind either – as long as we were all helping the war effort, what did it matter if our few letters were late in delivery, or that the postman missed a couple of halves in the pub because he was stuck on the other side of the river, nobly drinking tea?

The spring following my attack of jaundice found me fifteen years old and unemployed. Then Mrs Seymour asked if I'd like to help in the shop again for the summer. This year things were different: I was better-looking and therefore more confident – positively bold, some would say. So I went along happily and even enjoyed it.

Mrs Seymour was a pretty, petite blonde with plenty of will-power and nerves of steel. We thought she looked like Joan Blondel, Joan Bennett and all the other blonde film stars of the day (and there were a lot of them!) She was also prone to exaggeration and possessed a wicked sense of humour. Flitting about on her tiny four inch heels, she made me feel gauche and huge. She teased Edna and me alarmingly, as we blushingly served strange soldiers with cigarettes by the front door, shrieking witty innuendoes from the safety of the kitchen.

The house and cafe were adjacent to the tow path of the river and one day a large rat ran into the kitchen and through into the scullery. Mrs Seymour was at the ready; she armed Edna and me with brooms and instructions to stand by and hit the rat as it came out. She then went into the scullery banging saucepan lids and the frightened rat rushed out.

"Hit it, hit it," she shouted, to no avail. Edna and I were by then perched on top of the kitchen table, clutching one another in fear. Mrs Seymour was disgusted at our feeble attempts.

At this time, petrol tankers from Bristol travelled through, taking their cargo to Stourport. While passing through the lock, some of the men would nip down the river-side to fetch cigarettes, which were in very short supply and to which the local men were given priority. It was almost like a ration. My father smoked forty Woodbines a day, much to the disgust of Mother, who said he should sacrifice his smoking in wartime.

"Am I to have no pleasures?" said Dad, darkly.

"Pleasure?" "Ha!" said Mother.

Anyway, Edna and I had our special favourites amongst the tanker men. We both liked "Red Beret" and "Greasy-tug-boy" and always scrabbled and fought to answer the door to them. If we were seated at the table during meal-times, the one facing the window could see who was approaching or even see the name of the tanker as it passed by. This involved a lot of cheating and more scrabbling to get the coveted chair, so eventually we had to work out a fair arrangement and would kick one another under the table to indicate when one of our favourites was approaching.

Mr Seymour, unaware of this ethical situation, would often "cop" a sharp kick on the leg by mistake and glare suspiciously at us girls, while his spouse giggled happily, being party to the arrangement.

We made a lot of friends among the boat-men. The old steam tugs *Active* and *Victor* were then in operation, under "Uncle" Eric and his nephew Lee from Gloucester. They usually managed to arrive in time to tie up by the landing stage of the local pub and would sail off the next morning.

The summer ended and with it my job.

One Monday morning in September, I was "hanging" about in the garden and Mother was doing the washing in the wash-house, singing 'Cheri-Beri-Bin' as she usually did on wash day, and rolling her "r's" like Arthur Tracy, the street singer – whom *she* said was Irish, but I now find was of Russian extraction – and Cavan O'Conner, who was definitely Irish. Up the road slowly cycled a tall elderly lady with pink cheeks, on a tall bicycle (a "sit up and beg" we called them).

She was wearing a long tartan skirt, tweed jacket, brogue shoes and a felt hat. She leapt off her bicycle and smiled beamingly at me, saying: "I am Miss MacDonald, the matron from the school which has been evacuated to the castle. Is there anyone in your family who would like a little work sweeping and dusting dormitories, *quite* light work?"

At that moment, round the yard from the wash-house came Mother, wearing her overall, scarf, woolly hat, Dad's rubber boots (it was always dank and cold in the wash-house), and her usual autumn cold-sore adorning her upper lip like a moustache.

When she saw Miss MacDonald, all smart and upper-class, she looked nonplussed and attempted to quickly remove the cascade of clothes-pegs that were festooning her apron front. Miss MacDonald explained again, beaming encouragement every inch of the way.

The outcome was that I went to work at the castle and later, Mother went too, sewing and mending the sheets and children's clothes. I worked from nine till four, half a day on Saturday and two hours on Sunday. I earned ten shillings (50p) a week, with lunch thrown in.

At the suggestion of Miss MacDonald, I used to arrive at work fifteen minutes early in order that I could take part in the small morning service for the school given in the great hall.

CHAPTER 4

THE CASTLE

Although most people were not "into" history as they are today, I was intrigued by old buildings and found working at the castle very interesting.

The bedrooms were divided into sleeping accommodation with four to six beds per room. I was given the top floor, which had previously been the servants' quarters. The rooms were tiny and dusty (which started me with hay fever), and I used to have to sweep around with a broom and a mop under the beds and collect and carry all the little mats down the two staircases for shaking outside. I later devised a method, when the school was away, of hurling the mats through the tiny tower window and watching them sail through the air and plummet far away onto the ground below! No one came near me while I was working, so if the room looked clean and tidy, I could hang around day-dreaming

In most rooms was a wash-basin and I also had to clean the bathrooms.. Every Monday morning, the work brigade lined up in the kitchen and were given half a jar of *Vim* and a piece of soap measuring two square inches that looked and smelled like cheddar cheese. We were also given a linen tea-towel to polish off the basins at the end of the operation. Then I was allocated two rooms in the tower to sweep and dust, and up the spiral stone stairs I'd pant, with dust-pan and broom, to collapse exhausted on the bed of the French Mademoiselle – who was never about. I had a great time trying on her size eight shoes, cramming *both* my feet into one shoe, and sniffing and testing her *Elizabeth Arden* talc and perfume, sometimes assisted by Audrey, the house maid (who happened to be passing). We would lie on the bed and make plans for the evening's entertainment.

The school was a high-brow girl's boarding school from Sussex, with approximately 120 staff and pupils. The whole establishment was cared for by two matrons, one cook, one kitchen-maid, two parlour-maids, two gardeners, a "tweeny" and me. From time to time, domestic staff went off to do war work and whatnot; then the teaching staff and pupils would have to help out, washing up, laying tables and doing some of their own rooms. At one time there was only Alice (the "tweeny"), the kitchen maid and me, to take on the work load, which then had to consist mainly of preparing and delivering the food to the dining room.

At twelve o'clock every day, I would go downstairs to lay the tables and carry in the lunch, afterwards returning the plates and dishes to the kitchen while I washed the cutlery, beakers and glasses in the parlour-maids' pantry – though the social scene was changing rapidly, efforts were still being made to cling to the old class system. We still alluded to "parlour-maids and their pantries", and "house-maids and their pantries". The girl pupils were referred to by the staff as "the young ladies", or "Miss so and so", or "the Honourable Miss so and so". Later, one of our comrades, the afore-mentioned Audrey, caused a minor revolution when she said: "Those blinkin' kids had better watch out."

"Tut tut, Audrey," Miss MacDonald said, "You must not refer to the young ladies in that manner," and her poor soft pink face would twitch with anxiety.

"Well, they're no better than me – blinkin' kids!!"

"Hoity-toity, Audrey," – really flustered by this time.

After a little more rebellious repartee, Audrey said: "Take a month's notice."

"There, there, Audrey." And Miss MacDonald hurried away up the corridor to escape, as workers were hard to come by, leaving us envious domestics rolling about with laughter at Audrey's audacity.

Another revolution occurred when the Welsh contingency arrived – Mary and her little blonde sister Beryl, and Irene. Irene was a very tall, flashing-eyed brunette from South Wales, who taught us the Welsh National Anthem, the words of the latest popular songs, the Morse code and a bit more anarchy. She used to use spring-cleaning, an event which took place three times a year while the school was closed, as an opportunity to further our education.

For spring-cleaning, we all joined forces together; Freda, the kitchen-maid, did her province alone, the rest of us tackled the whole building. The library was not a popular place: we were expected to take down all the books and bang them together to remove all the dust. As we sneezed and spluttered, Irene would stand on top of the step-ladder, with poker in hand, and recite Shakespeare. *Hamlet* and *Romeo and Juliet* were the favourites. We also acted out parts from various books, like *The Shooting Of Dan McGrew*, with sound effects added, and we re-cremated Sam McGee. Another thing Irene used to do was to study the dictionary to find new and mysterious words; these we would nonchalantly sprinkle into our conversation henceforth.

Spring-cleaning the great hall was a gigantic task. We had to line up (like in the army) and scrub our way across the stone floor in relays. To break the monotony, we had a special song for the occasion:

You are always in my heart,
Scrub scrub scrub scrub,

Even though we're far apart,
Scrub scrub scrub scrub (tango rhythm)

Ever after, we called it 'The Scrubbing Song'.

Lunch in the maids' room, the dingiest and muckiest-looking place you could ever see, was usually ghastly. Cook didn't consider it part of her duty to satisfy the taste buds of the domestic staff, so we used to get all the leftovers thrown together: days' old stew for instance, with beetroot and white sauce piled on top. We did enjoy cauliflower "au gratin"; but sometimes these little niceties would be spoiled by Freda's lolling in the doorway, "regaling" us with a tale of a dead rat she had found drowned in a jug of gravy; which, she said, would no doubt be served up for dinner tomorrow.

The teaching staff were a varied bunch. The German Jewess, Miss Schmidt, who later married an English soldier, was a very attractive lady; she had a head of black curls that I *greatly* envied; the "Mademoiselle"; and one teacher who was as near a man as could be, with tweeds, brogues, collar and tie and and Eton crop; of course, we had never heard of Lesbians, then. Then there was the young sports mistress, Miss Phipps, a very popular person who always "forgot" that she had seen the domestic staff (not allowed out after ten o'clock) at one of the local American hops. Another young mistress I remember, slept pillowless – a curative measure for her treble chins!

The cook was our anathema. She was almost an exact replica of Giles' grandmother, with thin, blonde, tightly cork-screwed curls, kept rigidly in place by a thin blonde hairnet; she was quite old so I think she must have been dragged out of retirement by the curlers.

There we would be, launched well and truly into a fine chorus of 'My Brother Sylvest', and the door would fly open to reveal the squat cook, her red face quivering and exploding with rage.

"Never in 'mai 'laif," she'd say (she came from Yorkshire),

"'ave I 'eard such a noise, ai'm sure the young ladies can hear you."

"Do 'em good", said Audrey, "Flippin' kids."

"Now, Audrey, you must not refer to the young ladies 'laik' that," said Cook. "Aive' never heard such cheek."

"Give us a kiss." Audrey would say, or – "Take a month's notice." And so the revolution went on, until one afternoon when unsuspecting Irene pushed the tea-trolly into the drawing-room. Wearing no stockings as she hadn't any – stockings unfortunately required coupons which we were all short of, to say nothing of money – she incurred the wrath of the Headmistress.

"Do not come to work again without them," she scolded.

So she didn't! She packed her bag and caught the first train back to Wales, pausing only to write a blistering but polite note, pointing out the fact that at the beginning of the war, no doubt the Headmistress and staff had probably managed to hoard many pairs of stockings, whilst she, Irene, and comrades, could not afford to do so. I'm sure the Headmistress, who was usually a fair and democratic person, admired her for this gesture.

So Irene departed and went to work in a factory in Wales, where she met and married her husband, Howard and lived happily ever after.

CHAPTER 5

GALLIVANTING

When I was seventeen and had been working at the castle for about two years, I had a bad dose of 'flu, twice, followed by tonsilitis. All in all I was in bed for some weeks and looked a pretty poor, weak wretch.

We had then a lovely doctor, who hadn't been, and wasn't with us for long, Dr Pawson. He called to see me many times and sympathised that I had to be confined to bed in springtime – in those days, we had never heard of twenty-four or forty-eight hour 'flu, and a bout meant at least two weeks in bed. One day he called in with a bunch of primroses that he had picked for me along the side of a lane. What a wonderful thing for a G.P. to do! He recognised my frustration at being parted from the countryside at this, the loveliest time of the year.

When I had sufficiently recovered, my Auntie Nell wrote to ask if I would like to go and stay with her at Pagham in Sussex. I certainly would, thank you, I told her. At this time she was living in a rented bungalow by the sea, in charge of three-year-old Rose, while Rose's mother was visiting her terminally ill husband in a nursing home at Leamington.

It was a great adventure for me. Dad took my case to the village on his bicycle and left it overnight in Mrs Perkins' shed. Mrs Perkins,

Dad's cousin on his mother's side, kept a sweet shop and stored bicycles for people who caught the bus into town. She charged twopence a week. Her husband was a respected thatcher; he was also the village barber. He used to cut the men's hair so short that we wondered if he used his thatching shears to do it. We didn't like Dad having such a short cut – he hadn't got much hair to play around with, anyway. When he came back nearly bald we used to make jokes like: "Hello! Another convict's escaped."

"I don't care what you say," said Dad huffily, "It's a damned good sixpenn'uth."

So off I went on the train to Paddington. I was very nervous, never having been on a train on my own before, and rarely on a train at all! We had usually travelled by coach to Portsmouth and Weston Super-Mare. The first time we went to Portsmouth, I was seven years old. The train had huffed and steamed noisily, and smelt of smoke and boiled eggs. At a station before Oxford it had filled up with very strange people, obviously going to a carnival. Next to me, crammed close with his bare brown arms touching mine, sat a Red Indian brave, with a lone feather, beaded skirt, armbands, bow and arrow – the lot. All the time he was plastering himself with brown make-up out of a tin and glaring at me (I thought). I was terrified of him.

This time – no Indians, red or otherwise, but instead, a train packed with servicemen. As I sat down, a New Zealander R.E.M.E. (Royal Electrical Mechanical Engineer) leaped to his feet and put my case on the rack.

Auntie Nell met me at Paddington and we spent a few hours in London sight-seeing. It was very quiet that day, hardly any traffic, with sand-bags and air-raid precautions prominent – but the air-raids had ceased by then.

First on the agenda was a visit to Westminster Abbey and a look at the grave of the unknown warrier; I remember wondering if it was

Uncle Jack Taylor, who had been killed in the First War. Lying on the grave was a wreath of flowers, placed there the previous day by the American Ambassador, presumably Joseph Kennedy (we knew nothing about the famous Kennedys, then).

After a snack at a Lyons Corner House, and a chocolate cake in Kunzles ("You must experience a Kunzels' cake," said Auntie).

We caught the train from Waterloo to Bogner, walked through a posh-looking estate at Aldwich where Randolf Churchill and other celebrities lived; then took the bus to Pagham.

I spent a lot of time on the beach with Rose that holiday, getting healthy and brown. I went into Bognor on the bus to the cinema and agreed, along with George V, that it was a very dull place ("Bugger Bognor," etc).

Rose's mother came to stay for a while – sleeping on the floor in the dining room, as other guests were occupying the bedrooms; and during this time, Auntie Nellie and me went off to Portsmouth for two weeks. We travelled by coach from Bognor, passing through Cosham and glimpsing the house where Charles Dickens was born.

I had loved Portsmouth so much as a child. It was still lovely to me now, but the bombing had devastated the centre of the town. I was pleased to see that Peter Verochio's ice-cream parlour was still in operation in the square opposite the Town Hall.

We stayed in a boarding-house kept by an elderly man and his son, and shared a large feather bed (not with the elderly man and son, I'll add). Breakfast was brought up to us on a tray by the son: bacon and dried egg – fritters mostly, with fried tomatoes, fried bread and a pot of tea. He also brought a jug of water for washing, since we did not have access to a bathroom. Breakfast would be followed by a day of sight-seeing and lazing on the beach.

Twice we went over to the Isle-of-Wight on the steamer, landing at Rhyde pier. I met a sailor from Dagenham. His name was Bill and I arranged to meet him in Southsea the following Sunday. He had just come back from abroad so was allowed to wear a white top to his sailor's hat, as opposed to the standard wartime navy blue. We duly met at the South Parade Pier and saw a show – Eric Winstone and his orchestra, with singer Alan Kane, who was also in uniform. Later, we took a bus to Fareham and had a drink in the Red Lion. I quite liked this sailor and promised to write to him.

Every day, Auntie Nell and I went to one of the British Restaurants for lunch. These were wartime utility eating houses, rather like canteens, established and run by voluntary workers to provide cheap meals. The cooked lunch was one shilling (5p) and was quite sufficient.

We went to the King's theatre and saw Celia Lipton and Billy Milton in *The Quaker Girl* – Celia Lipton was the daughter of Sydney Lipton, who was a famous dance band leader then, a fact which greatly impressed me.

We saw two variety shows at the Coliseum, with a promising young ventriloquist performing – Peter Brough and his dummy Archie Andrews. We also saw song writer, Art Noel, author of many popular songs of the day which I knew well, and Auntie Nellie not at all (she lived in a much more high-brow world than me).

One Sunday we went to a service in the Naval Church. We were the only civillians out of a packed congregation. It was pouring with rain when the service was finished, and a Naval Officer (Auntie said he must be an Admiral because of the rings on his sleeve – she knew about these things!) offered us a lift home in his car; we gracefully declined and I've always regretted it!

When the holiday was over, I travelled as far as london with two friends who were also staying at the bungalow. We did the usual things: St. Pauls' this time, me dragging my heavier case up to the Whispering Gallery; then home to resume work again and pick up with all the flirtations that I'd left on the simmer.

During that summer, the sailor from the Isle-of-Wight turned up to see me, hoping to encourage me into a more permanent relationship; he stayed the weekend, but by then I'd gone off him! He didn't seem so attractive without his white-topped hat and, in any case, I'd got other fish to fry.

I remember going to meet him at the station accompanied by four other girl friends. He didn't go much on this, but it was the standard practice if our affections were on the wane, and anyway, the others all wanted to give him the "once over" in case there were any pickings in it for them. I tell you we were quite ruthless!

We stayed at Leamington once with Auntie Nell and Rose. Leamington was Rose and family's natural habitat and it was there that we met and talked to our first Yank. He was fat, dark, smart, smooth, clean, polite – and very nice.

We also stayed with various friends in Birmingham, particularly with Little Flo, near the gas works at Alum Rock. There, I bought my first nylon stockings, off a Jewish gent with the nose to prove it. Birmingham I thought a pretty awful place – too busy, all noise and tramcars. Our visits mostly incorporated "doing" a show. The Hippodrome was a popular venue; there we saw Big Bill Campbell's *Rocky Mountain Rhythm*, Cyril Fletcher and Betty Astell, May West in *Diamond Lil'*, and my greatest *current* hero Monte Rey and Jack Jackson and his band, with a pianist named Bruce Forsyth!

One year, three of us spent a week with Irene at her home in Pontllanfraith. Irene's father was a Welsh miner, while her Mother was from London. During our holiday there, we met lots of Dais and Yantos, but not one of Rene's three brothers, who were all away fighting. We took rides around the mountain in Willie "the bread's" van, who had teeth as black as the coal that surrounded him. I'm sure he felt a "hell of a fella" with all us girls hanging around him! One day when we were out with him, we watched a house blazing on the other side of the mountain. We were powerless

6.0 • TWICE NIGHTLY FOR TWO WEEKS COMMENCING MONDAY, APRIL 1st, 1946 • 8.15

LESLIE A. MacDONNELL

presents

MAYFAIR MERRY-GO-ROUND

Special Songs and Material by Dick Hurran and Jack Jackson

Orchestrations by Jack Jackson

Dances arranged by Barbara Aitken

1 **OVERTURE**

2 **THE MERRY-GO-ROUND COMES TO TOWN**

The Mayfair Tiller Girls
Ted Fielding
Jack Jackson
Anna Mac
Owen McGiveney
Syd & Max Harrison
Monte Rey
Jack Jackson's Band

3 **SYD & MAX HARRISON**

have a few words to say

4 **OWEN McGIVENEY**

The World's Greatest Quick-Change Artiste in "BILL SIKES"

5 **"THE WAGER" ?**

6 **"SHINING SHOES"**

ANNA MAC and THE GIRLS

7 **JACK JACKSON and his BAND**

PERSONNEL :

JACK JACKSON	Conductor
Clem Stevens	1st Trumpet
Dennis Townsly	2nd Trumpet
Bill Sharp	Trombone
Ronnie Austin	1st Alto Sax.
Glyn Taylor	2nd Alto Sax.
Johnny Roberts	Tenor Sax.
Ted Shuttleworth	Bass
Barney Gilbraith	Accordion
Bruce Forsyth	Piano
Leslie Roy	Drums

8 **INTERMISSION—**

Selection : "Perchance to Dream"
THE HIPPODROME ORCHESTRA
directed by KEVIN MALLON

9 **THE MAYFAIR TILLER GIRLS**

10 **ANOTHER SPOT OF FUN**

11 **MONTE REY**

Radio's Romantic Singer
At the Piano : FRANK PALESON

12 **"JUST NUTS"**

SYD & MAX HARRISON

13 **THE MERRY-GO-ROUND FINALE**

By the ENTIRE COMPANY

Manager ...... TED FIELDING
Musical Director ...... HAL BEVAN
(For LESLIE A. MacDONNELL)

to help as it was miles away, so we could only hope it was empty.

We also went on a day trip to Barry. We started out at about six, running across fields to catch the train at the junction, and had to change trains at Cardiff. Though it was only thirty miles away, the journey took us hours. How pampered we are today. To have a day out then took a fair bit of effort. Perhaps this made us appreciate it more – I hope so.

We were thrilled to be in a "foreign" capital. We saw our first Black American, strolling around with large cigars at the ready, and went to the fair, picking up some Yankee soldiers on the way (white), who paid for us to go on the dodgems and the switch-back. A good time was had by all!

I suppose working in a school did at least mean we had long paid holidays – about six weeks a year, which was a lot in the days when most people only qualified for one week. So, wartime or not, I managed quite a bit of time away. Gallivanting, Dad called it, begrudgingly.

CHAPTER 6

THE ITALIANS

We were quite prepared to hate the Italian prisoners when we heard that they were to be housed in the nearly constructed camp at Hampton Lovatt. We were going to be indifferent, ignoring, oblivious and uncaring. After seeing so many news reels of the smiling, happily surrendering, cowardly little "Eyeties" in the Middle East, we felt utter contempt for them and boo-ed them enthusiastically at the cinema.

These feelings, however, were only a temporary state of affairs. I suppose you could say that like the Ceasars of their day, they came, they saw and, with their cheerful personalities and good looks, they conquered us. They were so handsome – black curly hair, shining eyes, little moustaches, little square hands – that we soon found them impossible to ignore.

In their dark brown uniforms, waving, cheering and blowing kisses, they used to pass our house every morning and night as the lorries took them to work on the farms. We took great pains to be outside when they passed, so that we could glare at them, or stick our noses in the air. "Ah! Carrisima," they yelled, "we love you." In the end, we succumbed and laughed with, and at them.

Very soon they were allowed to live on the farms, and then even to fraternise *slightly* with the villagers. They got hold of some old bicycles and pedalled around, rolling their eyes at any female they met. Soon we were chatting happily away to them. They were not allowed in the pubs at first, and were restricted by curfews, so this meant that if they were still chatting to us after eight o'clock at night, our policeman Mr Shaylor would pedal slowly up the road on his bike and glare at them.

In our district, we had Felix and Leo, Nici and Luigi, Joseph and Amletto and Tony and Yotsi. Yotsi was our favourite. He was small and square, with green eyes and very handsome. He loved all the girls and regularly told them so.

The Italians had a particular scent: warm and heavy, a cross between hot tea and spice. Yotsi would stroll nightly along the road on the lookout for girls to talk to. "I love you," he'd say, "You love me? You like to marry me?"

Naturally, the first English taught to him by his workmates consisted largely of swear words. So then he would say: "You bl . . . y lovely girl", or – "I love you, you b . . . r." We soon trained him out of that, although it was quite amusing at the time.

One Italian, Amletto, carried an English Phrase book around with him and, as we approached, would look up suitable things to say. He had a terrific crush on our friend, Irene, who was six feet tall. Little Amletto was a very serious Italian, and as he gazed passionately into Irene's kneecaps, would say – via his phrase book: "It is fatty (fate) that we meet like this." He was completely astonished when we shrieked and rolled around with laughter; his black eyes smouldered and he looked quite dangerous.

Normally, my father didn't approve of us talking to the Italians. Then one day, little Yotsi was hanging over the gate, rolling his big eyes and telling us girls how beautiful we were, as usual, when Mrs White, a lady who had a weekend bungalow by the river, came walking down the road. She stopped and stared at Yotsi and said bitterly: "You're living like lords in this country, while my son is in a German prison camp, starving to death. You ought to have the same treatment." And looking at us – "People should be ashamed to be seen talking to you!"

Well! Yotsi was astonished and naturally could not understand this unfair treatment. After all, he didn't start the bl . . . y war, he told us, tears streaming down his face. That Mussolini! no bl . . . y good, the bugger ought to be shot with that Hitler. *He was* shattered.

At that moment Dad came round the yard agreeing with him. "He's only an ordinary working class chap like me," he explained, "He can't help what the fascists are doing."

This was as surprising to us as Mrs Whites' attack was to Yotsi! We stood dumbfoundedly gazing at Dad. After all, we'd been brought up on the basic fact that the only good German was a dead one and, at this moment in history, that applied to Italians as well.

From then on, Dad was pleasanter to the Italians: "Poor little sods," he'd say, "they're only human."

One old farmer, Mr Hodges, had an Italian working and living on his farm. A very fine looking fellow was Joseph. Old Hodges, who was a bachelor, wanted to adopt Joseph as his son, and begged him to come back after the war and make his home there, declaring he would leave him the farm and all his possessions. But Joseph, unfortunately, was determined to become a priest and declined the offer. The farm incidentally, was Clacks of Arthur Billet, B.B.C. fame.

After secretly courting for three years, my sister became engaged to an Italian – Adriano, whom we called Adrian. She was engaged for some time but a marriage never materialised, much to her sorrow. Adrian was not like the other Italians; the son of a diplomat in Tripoli, he was educated and soon spoke far better English than we did, producing words that we had never heard of! He was very aloof, especially with the other Italians and treated their silly endearing "little ways" with utter contempt.

I also had a few weeks' flirtation; Louigi, an Italian living in Madrid, had come hot-foot from the Spanish Civil War to join Mussolini's army. He was very nice and very handsome, but I too had to meet him in clandestine fashion, as I was only fifteen at the time.

So all in all we accepted the Italians as diversions and as misfits of the war. Quite a few settled in England and married local girls and those that didn't went back after the war to their homes and families. I wonder what they really thought about the English country people. I hope they had pleasant memories of us, as we did of them.

CHAPTER 7

HONEY, WASPS AND GERMANS

While we grew fond of the Italian prisoners, I think I can honestly say that we were never fond of the Germans. When the first German prisoners started to work on the farms, we were more adamant than *ever* that we were in no way going to fraternize with *them*. Our first "meeting" only furthered our convictions.

Wearing grey overcoats and grey peaked caps, they would crouch on the back of their lorries like large vultures, shoulders hunched, coat-collars turned up around their scowling unhappy faces, heads sunken as low as possible into their collars. With their cold, blue eyes they scowled at us and sometimes even spat at us. We hated them: they were so sinister, like a lorry-load of Conrad Viedts embarking on cruel wartime activities.

As the war progressed, the Germans settled into our slip-shod humanistic way and we made friends with a few of them, but we never "adopted" them on the chummy scale that we did the Italians.

My father didn't trust the Germans, the Italians or the French. Neither did he trust the Scots, the Irish and the Welsh. My mother didn't trust the French; she also didn't trust the bees and the wasps. An innocent buzz in the distance would convince her of trouble on its way.

So while Rupert Brook ate honey for his tea – we didn't. Mother didn't trust honey: she believed it a "suspicious" product, in spite of Auntie Nellie's trying to convince her how good it would be for our weakly bronchials. After all, wasn't it found in Tutankhamen's tomb, after *all those years* proving how pure it was? Mother wasn't satisfied: she didn't trust the Egyptians either!

Mother, a placid, kindly and good-tempered soul, was always so considerate to the underdog and to people and animals in trouble; but she did have her occasions of panic and mistrust. Our summer meal-times were frequently interrupted by Mother's leaping madly around with a rolled-up *Daily Express*, swatting at some unsuspecting wasp for all she was worth. In her attempts to catch it, she knocked over the milk; the bread and butter slid about haphazardly; the table-cloth flipped over, and we would be accidentally clouted over our heads, backs, arms and legs. Finally, Dad's "For God's sake! you'll have the tea off the table in a minute" would bring his impatience and irritability to the fore. It was an uncomfortable time for one and all. Poor Mother, she meant to render us such a service, but it would have been easier and quicker if one of us had volunteered for a *sting* and killed the poor wasp off that way!

Another great panic occurred whenever anyone lost a needle. Mother would turn the house upside down in her frenzy to find it; the reason being, she explained, that a friend of her sister Ethel, while nursing in a mental hospital, had died as a result of a needle penetrating her knee. Blood poisoning?

One night, during wartime, I woke up to find myself being humped downstairs by Mother, while she moaned hysterically: "They're trying to kill us all." She tossed me on the old sofa, threw a coat over me and I went back to sleep. A little later I was woken up to be dragged back up the stairs. That was the night a solitary bomb was dropped two miles away by a solitary German bomber; on his way home, he was probably panicking as much as Mother!

The day another bomb jettisoned over Worcester City, off went Mother with a coat over her apron, leaving everything scattered in her path, to catch the first bus into Worcester. She was convinced the Germans were trying to bomb "their" Harry. Uncle Harry did laugh when she arrived on his door step.

"Well, Mabs," he said, "you ought to know better. The Kaiser couldn't finish me off in the First War and I'm darned sure I'm not going to let Hitler do it for him!"

So he made her a nice cup of tea and Auntie Laura sent her back home on the next bus; incidentally, clutching a black hat that Auntie Laura didn't like, and a pair of old curtains that Auntie Laura didn't want – she was still convinced then that we were totally uncivilized in the country and didn't have any curtains.

CHAPTER 8

THE AMERICANS

Everyone awaited the arrival of the American G.I.s with great excitement. We understood from Dad that, though boastful, bragging – and late, they had entered the First War in time to save the Brits from further slaughter and cause the Germans to surrender. It was hoped they would do the same this time!

The first "sitings" were at Ashchurch, near Tewkesbury. In their off-duty hours, the soldiers were allowed into Worcester, and on our occasional visits to town, we would watch them strolling around, mostly looking very tall, or fat, in strange smooth uniforms, smoking long cigarettes or large cigars and wearing brown leather shoes, as opposed to the clumsy boots of our own soldiers.

It wasn't long before we heard of fights and stabbings at The Star Hotel between black and white Yanks – a situation completely alien to us. Then we heard that the blacks and whites were to be segregated for their off-duty periods. We also heard of local girls who followed the Yanks and got "pains under their pinnies" for their trouble.

Parents were naturally dubious. But then, in the May of that year, one of our most delightful springs when the countryside was beautiful and all the blossom out, a new batch of Americans arrived at Westwood Park, the home of Lord Doverdale. Unlike the others, these respected, indeed were thrilled with our country, and particularly with Lord Doverdale's being a *real* lord. They became "our Yanks" and we were very attached to them. Almost without exception, they were good-mannered, good-natured and friendly; they were even forgiven for invading and taking over the local pubs. We had a great time with them.

They used to have little books instructing them how to behave in England and went to great pains to refuse any food or drinks offered by the near-starving Brits. They admired us extremely for our fortitude in holding out against Hitler and were astonished that we were so cheerful on our short food rations. We laughed at them and insisted that they partake of our bread, cheese, pickles and homemade wine. As they relaxed, they entered our homes and we all became very "chummy". Of course, having no previous knowlege of Americans, excepting our pet American Mr Charles Devine and the voice of Paul Robeson, we still had the idea that they were all either millionaires, cowboys or film stars.

One day, my sister proffered her autograph book to one of the G.I. visitors, a Johnny Franks. We were astonished to find that he could only just write his name. He sat at our table, elbows akimbo, tongue in cheek, concentrating hard on writing out the letters "JOHN A. FRANKS". It took him ages. Well, that was an eye opener, I can tell you!

They were so generous the Yanks, doling out not one, but whole packets of cigarettes: *Camel, Lucky Strike* ("Pity I don't like that sort," said Dad regretfully); also, chewing gum by the packet, and bags of sweets and chocolate for the children.

We made special friends with Steve Sordyl, Big Ed, Donald D. Splitlog and Johnny Franks. Their names caused quite a bit of hilarity. Johnny Halzapple Norton West, we always referred to as North, South, East and West. They sounded so strange, after our own ordinary names. There was also Johnny O'Sullivan, who piloted a little trainer plane; he used to circle over our cottage very low, just above the telegraph wires, and wave to us.

Dances were organised at the local hotel-cum-pub, with refreshments and drinks provided. Everybody would be invited. An American army dance band would play our national anthem; and 'John Brown's Body', which throughout our childhood had been "a-mouldering in the grave", suddenly resurrected itself and became: 'Mine Eyes Have Seen The Glory etc.'. Yes! we were all terribly nice to each other.

The only ripple of discontent came from our own servicemen, who, when home on leave, found their homes invaded and their girl friends' and sisters' affections stolen. Some of them grew very bitter, which was understandable: while the Yanks were over here having a good time and prancing around with the local girls, many of them had been in serious action abroad.

No doubt the girls were attracted by their smooth uniforms (anyone who has been clasped to the bosom of an English sailor's rough uniform will know what I mean), smooth talk and smooth hands, to say nothing of their lucrative spending money.

With the coming of the G.I.s, new words materialised, such as "vest" for waistcoat and "closet" for cupboard (Mother always referred to our lavatory as "the closet"). The Americans couldn't understand this "fortnight" we talked about." Why don't you say two weeks?" they said. We had no idea – do we now?

Some people exploited the G.I.s and would overcharge them for goods in shops. The Yanks at Westwood were keen to get bicycles to ride down to various pubs and villages. Bicycles were almost impossible to come by then, and they were sold all sorts of crocks. Big Ed rode up on a tradesmen's delivery bike; he had sawn off the large basket holder at the front and was just left with the little wheel, which looked ridiculous. Then Steve turned up on a rusty old bike; his friends decided to brighten it up for him and one night painted it in rainbow coloured stripes. It was a laugh! He didn't mind though; it got him around, creaking and groaning every Saturday night up to the local pub, all of six miles away, just to hear Leslie, or "Less" as he pronounced it, playing his request – 'The Indian Love Call.'

The G.I.s were also called "dough-boys". Was it because they had so much money to spend, or was it to do with dough-nuts? – at this time milk bars were coming into being in the towns throughout England, and everywhere windows invited us in big letters to "Come in! and dunk a Doughnut". Once again an appropriate song appeared –

Let's have a tiddly at the milk bar,
Let's make a night of it tonight,
Let's have a tiddly at the milk bar,
Let's paint the town a creamy white,
You have half a pint,
I'll have half a pint,
You've got to have a pint somehow so –
Let's have a tiddly at the milk bar,
And drink to the dear old cow!

What we found particularly strange about the Americans was their enthusiasm, a characteristic rarely found in the English. They pursued girls with untiring vigour and at the drop of a hat – or anything else – they launched into proposals of marriage, usually sincere!

One night I was strolling along the road on my way home, when I met up with a very young G.I. He walked along with me towards home and in the space of perhaps five minutes, he had told me his name was Paul Jennings, where he lived, all about his home and parents and asked whether I was interested in marrying him.

Well, I quickened my pace, suspecting something queer in all this. He pleaded with me and begged me until I turned round and walked back with him (I didn't fancy turning up on the doorstep with such an odd-bod). Together we paced up and down the road, backwards and forwards over the bridge, until he was finally persuaded that I was not going to give in to him. I thought he was a bit crazy, but I heard shortly after that he had actually persuaded a local girl to marry him; she went out to America with him after the war and produced eight children, so I wasn't sorry that I hadn't encouraged him!

After the Americans left to serve with the 3rd Army and General Patton, we kept in touch with many of them. Don Splitlog wrote to my mother for years from Detroit, but we never saw any of them again.

We also became attached to the American stars who entertained us on the radio – Bebe Daniels, Ben Lyon, Vic Oliver, who married Mr Churchill's daughter Sarah. How we loved them and listened and laughed with them –*Bing Sings* – we used to have Bing Crosby's special fifteen minute programmes several times a day; likewise Charlie Kunz' *Clap Hands, Here Comes Charlie.* We adored them both, and throughout the war they sustained and boosted our so-called low spirits.

Every week there was a quiz show on the radio, *Penny On The Drum,* in which a very excitable American, Clay Keys, with mounting hysteria, asked competing couples musical questions such as: "What did one bear say to the other?" Answer: "Amapola" – a pop song of the day; or – "What did the exasperated husband say to his wife, as he sat down to dinner?" Answer: "Whale meat again?" (We were very fond of whale meat jokes).

As the programme progressed and competitors guessed the right tune, Clay Keys became more and more excited and screamed and shrieked with fervour. As the band – equally excited – blasted out the correct tune, one could imagine the very instruments trembling and steaming with emotion. It was all a bit daft but we enjoyed it; it was also part of the great "Jolly Along The Brits" campaign. We were grateful to the friendly Americans but we didn't need that much cheer; after all, we were still *Great Britain*, weren't we?

CHAPTER 9

THE HOME GUARD

The Home Guard were, on the whole, an admirable band of men and boys: some did a hard day's work on the land, in all weathers – and land work wasn't as mechanised as it is today, others cycled the seven to twelve miles into town and back, six days a week; then all would have to turn out at night to aid the war effort and defend the rural areas. I wonder, would the youth of Britain do the same now? The vicar at one of our local churches remarked in the Parish magazine:

> *A word in conclusion about our Home Guard. The change in the weather has not deterred them. They carry out their nightly duties despite storm and tempest, frost and cold. Whether or no the danger of Invasion has passed, it gives one a feeling of security to know that L.D.V. is unceasingly vigilant. Good luck to 'em, and good health.*

When they were first formed, the Home Guard was known as the Local Defence Volunteers, or L.D.V., and we locals tended to scorn and laugh at the whole idea. "Phaw!" said Dad, "I'd like to see old Bert H . . . if he actually came up against a German. He'd mess his trousers! (. . . not a bit like *they* were in the First War! etc.)" We thought it amusing to see our former school mates, not long school leavers, together with some of the more "daddicky" old men, marching up and down smartly – or trying to march up and down smartly, with the appointed sergeant fiercely barking out orders. Once again, we would loll by the railings over the field where they did their training, giggling as usual, the sergeant glaring at us and no doubt wishing that we would clear off. The ridicule continued until they were given uniforms and became the efficient "Home Guard" – we realized they really meant business!

I composed a song about them. Sung to the tune of 'Around The Marble Arch', it went like this:

Across the bridge they march,
Their legs as stiff as starch,
What a wonderful sight to see,
All the pick of the L.D.V.,
The sergeants in the rear,
The folks begin to cheer,
What a glorious sight to see,
Our local L.D.V!

When Mr Seymour, who later became a lieutenant, wasn't about, I substituted "cheer" for "jeer", which made my mates laugh heartily. George Formby also joined me in singing –

I'm guarding the home of the Home Guard,
I'm guarding the Home Guard's home.

The Home Guard's hut, where they met nightly, was at the bottom of the road, next to our long garden; and we were the proud recipients of The Key. Every night, the sergeant marched up the road to our gate, sprang smartly to attention, saluted and handed us over the key; we would then hang it proudly up on the brush compendium by the door, in company with the bakers' books, the insurance books, any other keys and the fox's brush. We felt it an honour to be guardians of this key, and one of us would always be at home to receive it.

One of the home guards, sometimes boldly, sometimes shyly would call for the key and then Sergeant L– would complete The Ceremony of the Keys. After the Home Guard had dispersed, some went on duty to various posts in the district, some went home and some nipped off smartly to the pub, where they stayed until closing time and, money and quantity of beer allowing, got plastered.

One, who shall remain nameless, spent much of his time in an inebriated state. One night, when a visiting officer was expected, he got so drunk he had to be locked into the hut's lavatory to avoid being seen; he was kept there in happy oblivion, until it was safe to let him out! Another night, he woke to find himself in an A.T.S. girl's bed, at the Norbury Hotel in Droitwich! – the A.T.S. Girl was not in the bed at the same time, I hasten to add.

Dad couldn't bear to see this chap approaching. He had a habit of falling sideways off his bike, and into Dad's immaculately-cut hedge. We girls were always hauling him out: "Don't you encourage that b . . . ," Dad would say, "He'll finish up at the end of a rope."

Occasionally, the Home Guard had to carry out manoeuvres on a grand scale, and would converge on our little hamlet from many platoons in the area. A great mass of men and lorries appeared one night, with instructions to conduct a mock battle by the river, defending and guarding the bridge. All kinds of bangs and crashes and flashes went on and heads kept appearing over the hedge and from behind trees. Later on, as I was gazing out of my bedroom window into the moonlit night, a voice shouted up at me: "What about a date?" I couldn't see the owner of the voice properly, so had no idea what he looked like: how could I say no? At least he *sounded* passable, so I agreed and the next night he turned up on his bike.

It had seemed a very romantic notion at the time, a voice in the moonlight, but on seeing him I changed my mind. Carrying a raincoat over his arm (with no ulterior motive, I'm sure), he was very young, terribly shy and continually blushing. We went for a walk and didn't say a word all the time. When we reached a certain point, about a mile away, we turned and walked silently back. Then he jumped on his bike and was away home. I felt very foolish, especially as we had passed some of my friends who whistled and cat-called rudely at us. What silly things we did then! He wrote to me once, asking for another date, but I never saw him again. Sadly, I heard a long time after that he had been killed in the war.

Our Home Guard weren't a bad lot and we had great fun with some of them. We had two Johns and two Jacks in our local division. My friend Edna persisted in saying when we met them together: "Hello Jack, Hello John, Hello Jack, Hello John." We ragged her about this but she said: "Well, it's their names!" I said: "Why don't you say: 'hello all?'" but she wouldn't have that.

The night the Home Guard was disbanded, or "stood down" as they called it, there were high jinks in the neighbourhood. After a good booze-up, the men wended their wobbly way towards our house, where they marched up and down larking about. Then one of them decided to lie flat out in the middle of the road and another fell over him, landing head-first on the tarmac and cutting his head quite badly. At the time, we were just wishing good night by the gate to our friend Nellie, who was a nurse home on leave from London. Nellie dragged the confused soldier (one of the Jacks) into the house and bathed and plastered him in no uncertain terms. He "oo-ed" and "ar-ed" as she unmercifully poured generous dollops of iodine into the wound.

"Serves him right for drinking," said Nellie, who always

treated men with utter contempt. The rough treatment seemed to do Jack good, for he was soon recovered and chasing us girls round the table. The hanging lamp swayed and groaned on its chains as we dashed about – to the horror of Mother, who thought we would all catch fire or burn the house down, or both. We remembered for years the stand down of the Home Guard or rather the *fall* down, as we called it.

CHAPTER 10

EVACUEES AND A LITTLE RATIONING

There has been a saying knocking around for years, that the only fools in the country are the ones that come out from the towns. We true country people go along with this implicitly, and in some measure have been proved correct. With all the education and high technology of modern days, I think we still have more know-how as regards the correct treatment of the land and environment. This has been more than proven by the disasters of grubbing up hedges and trees; filling in ponds and ditches, or allowing them to become so blocked that the natural rainwater does not drain as it should; and allowing hedgeless fields and treeless spaces, which make for dust bowls and wind traps. The old footpath arguments, so relevant now, are also coming to fruition. We country-folk don't take kindly to townies informing us - incorrectly - where the old footpaths and roads used to be, especially since we walked most of them in our youth.

In the wartime we were astonished at the ignorance of the evacuees as regards food, and a way of life we took for granted. Many of them had no idea what went into the growing of cabbages and peas and beans; and the way they described vegetables! After all, we ate "sprouts" for our Sunday dinner, who'd ever heard of "Brussels"? (apart from the the First World War reminiscences of Dad and cronies, of course); or "Cox's" apples – they were "pippins" to us: orange, ribstone or herrings. Of course, things like courgettes and sweetcorn hadn't been invented then.

We did relax a little in the war, where food was concerned, enough to accept spam and dried egg. The jokes about spam were numerous. And jokes about being "conned" into eating whale meat – "Whale meet again," we laughingly sang with Vera Lynn and Clay Keys. We also sang: "It had to B.U." – B.U.s were the coupons we had for bread rationing (Bread Units).

The evacuee children obviously didn't understand our country nourishment, like "bread and cheese" from the hawthorn hedge and the sweet syrup we sucked from the white nettles. They were alarmed and thought we would be poisoned. In fact, the whole country system confused them. One girl who came to stay with her aunts, the Miss Scraggs, during the war, asked the number of our cottage, and said: "But all houses have numbers."

"Ours don't," we said scornfully. We didn't have avenues and streets and things, we told her, we lived "up the road", "down the road", "up the bank", "round the lane", "up the river", "down the river", "round the corner", "over there" – or "there!", "up the headland", "down the headland", "up the top barn", or "by the castle"!

Our mothers managed reasonably well on the rations. In the country we had vegetables in the garden, and there was always the odd rabbit to be got from one of Dad's mates. Sometimes we had dripping, flavoured with rosemary, or a bit of pig's liver or chitterlings from a neighbour's pig-killing.

There were many formalities to go through as regards keeping a pig. My friend Edna, was now working for the Ministry of Agriculture in Worcester, had hilarious tales to tell: "Dear Sir, my wife died recently so I have decided to keep a pig etc." And tales of old farmers with hair sprouting from their ears like wisps of corn, who had never been into town before, but went to get advice on their "hagricultural hosses".

If we found a Colorado beetle on our potatoes, we were promised a reward of five pounds, a vast sum. How we searched through the potato sacks for those poor little blighters!

Bananas were a popular commodity that almost completely disappeared during the war. We as a family had always eaten a lot of bananas as being "good for us". S.O.S. messages were often read out on the radio, appealing for them for children who were very sick with a certain condition (I wonder what?). We girls sat on the lock gates or on the wall of the bridge, and gloomily vowed that come the end of the war, we would stuff ourselves silly with bananas, we liked them so much. Sweets and chocolate were never a problem though, we had sufficient rations; in fact the rations were half a pound a month per person (I think), which ended up being more than we were allowed in peace time! Nevertheless, we young girls liked to think that we were "hard done by".

The most popular commodities on ration with our family were dried egg and golden syrup, the latter of which you could "do" a lot with: sweetening puddings etc.

When Dad got a job as fire-watcher at a timber yard by the river in Stourport, he found that boats being unloaded from Bristol and Gloucester, sometimes had mishaps, like burst sugar sacks. So he got permission to sweep up the gash sugar, dirt and all, and was gleefully able to continue his making wine with garden vegetables and hedgerow products.

As regards other rations, we managed quite well. Mother had always kept margarine in the house for cake and pastry-baking, but we *never* ate it on bread. To illustrate, once, in about the mid-Thirties, Dad had to go to Birmingham for a fitting: he needed a new pair of the surgical boots he always wore, owing to the severe leg wounds he had received in the Great War (the nerves in one leg being severed and causing the arch of the foot to drop). Mother went with him which was unusual while, Auntie Nell stayed with us children. On their return, Mother gasped in horror: "What is that margarine doing on the table?" and Auntie Nell replied that she couldn't find the butter so we had been eating it for tea. Mother was very alarmed and said: "I hope it won't upset them!"

Auntie Nell laughed and said: "Don't be silly, Mabs!" and Mother said "But we never eat it on bread." She was convinced we would suffer ill-effects and would watch us worriedly for some days, to see if anything developed.

That just shows what we thought of margarine in our family. I expect poorer families than ours ate it every day; if they were lucky enough to have even that. In the war things changed and we had to mix butter and margarine together, but Mother never took to marg. and she pushed it around the butter dish relentlessly, hoping it would disappear off the face of the earth and not worry her any more! Nothing substituted butter for her.

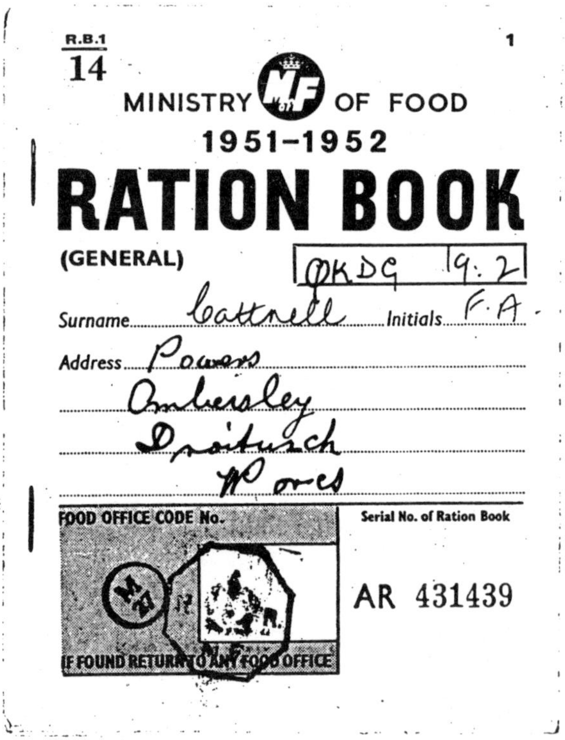

R.B.1
14

1

MINISTRY OF FOOD
1951–1952
RATION BOOK
(GENERAL)

QKDG 9.2

Surname Cattrell Initials F.A.

Address Powers
Ombersley
Droitwich
Worcs

FOOD OFFICE CODE No.

Serial No. of Ration Book

AR 431439

IF FOUND RETURN TO ANY FOOD OFFICE

CHAPTER 11

MEANWHILE, BACK AT THE WAR

Meanwhile, back at the war, Dad decided to take us all to see Charlie Chaplin in *The Great Dictator*. We were surprised and pleased at the news of this outing; going to the pictures involved walking a mile and a half either way to catch the bus into Worcester and it was unusual for Dad to want to go or to take us out. On Saturday, a bus passed by the door twice a day, but Dad decided to take us in the week to avoid the crowds (what crowds?). Dad had been a fan of Chaplin in the silent days, as well as of Al Jolson, whom he had seen in *The Singing Fool*. He never stopped singing the praises of Al Jolson and scoffed at our Gables, Colemans and Flynns.

During this time, new words and expressions came to our ears: "blitz", "armaments", "forty-eight hours leave", etc. Mr Wood, a neighbour, met a soldier who was on "Embrocation" (Embarcation) leave. Captain Peter Green, who had served in the army in the East had an Indian batman; (an officer's exclusive servant). Complete with turban and brass buttons, this batman used to talk to us girls over the gate (the gate was always a great talking place) and tell us he was going to "Kiddleleyminster" or "Birmingha'".

R.A.F. words, such as "wizard prang", "the drink", "bang on", "good show", "browned off", we heard mostly through Tommy Handley and his Wing-Commander Kite on the wireless, and air-force ground staff home on leave. New words like "sophistication" also entered our vocabulary and we strove to be it – sophisticated!

We had always had good blood, bad blood, thin blood and thick blood; now we had A.B.C. and Rhesus negative and that lot. "How humoresque," Mother would say (she had a good ear for words.) As we became hooked on General Montgomery, all our dogs were named Monty, as well as some of our canaries – budgerigars hadn't been heard of in our neck of the woods. Come to think of it, our local publican's name was Monty, too – how patriotic! Even our dog Paddy broadened his vocabulary: late at night when he was put out in his kennel to sleep, he would bark out words that sounded like war places or battles "Ber-rut", "El-Al-e-mein", "Too-bruk". Dad would go to the bedroom window and shout: "I'll warm your backside, lad, if you don't be quiet!"

Paddy, ever faithful, probably suspected that Hitler was lurking in the bushes. "Marshall Tim-i-shen-co," he would reply gruffly.

"That dog's as sensible as a Christian," said Dad fondly.

Our neighbour Mrs Passey used to talk to her hens as if they were her best friends, threatening to smack them if they didn't lay. She gave them all men's names: Edward, Peter, Harry and Percy, which, I remember, added further confusion to our sex education.

Dad and his cronies continued to grouse about the cost and scarcity of *Woodbines* and Fred Passey's *Twist Tobacco.*

"We ought to have finished 'em off in the last lot," said Dad darkly, referring to the Germans.

"Ah! lad. Ah! lad," replied his pals.

Dad got a little job: every Sunday morning he walked the fields by the river, which we call the Severn meadows and counted Mr Jackson's bullocks to see that none had gone astray. We called him Cowboy, or Gary Cooper. I think he liked that!

Meanwhile posters and adverts appeared everywhere, informing us that "Careless talk costs lives", and that we should "Be like Dad, keep Mum". We were cajoled into "digging for Victory", and asked: "Is your journey really necessary?" – we got laughs out of the last one, catching people on their way to the toilet etc.

By this time, we had all been issued with identity cards, with our own personal number. Mine was: QKDF 10-4.

"We're only numbers now," said Dad despairingly. "To think I went through the last war to end up like this."

When we reached a certain age, we had to sign the cards. When I received mine, I was still at the age of writing in a childish style. By fifteen I was very ashamed of this and, wanting to upgrade my image, I dropped a large blot of ink over my signature, covered it with stamp margin and wrote over it in a more grown-up hand. Later, when having to produce the card for security reasons, I was severely reprimanded for this. Mr Shaylor wasn't too pleased either: "It's a good thing I know you," he said, tongue-in-cheek.

We sometimes listened guiltily to the Lord Haw-Haw propaganda broadcasts in Berlin, (Lord Haw-Haw, alias William Joyce who was later executed as a spy). We thought them a laugh and would shout rudely at the wireless. Then an American, Quentin Reynolds, started broadcasting in a sort of tit-for-tat way. He had a deep, dark brown voice, which we tried to copy to the detriment of our throats. He said, if I can rightly recall, that Hitler's real name was Shicklegruber, and that he was a painter. We all thought he meant a house painter and henceforth, cartoons of Hitler in white overalls with brush, bucket and ladder splashing paint around, appeared in all the papers!

"We'll get you, Mister Shicklegruber," Quentin Reynolds would say, his voice sinking so deep that we expected to see his tonsils emerging through the bottom of the wireless.

As time went on, many more commodities became scarce. Soap was particularly difficult to come by. As I got older, and was allowed into town on my own, I remember once going into the chemists, George and Welsh, (now, alas, gone) and buying a tablet of lovely soap. It was wall-flower, a glorious perfume and anyone who has ever caught the scent of wallflowers in the rain, will know what I mean. It was eight pence (3½p) which was very expensive, but it sticks in my mind and nostrils, because it was so lovely and cost the same coupons per bar as the inferior soap we were getting. It probably lasted a year, as I only used it for best.

We weren't so obsessed with washing and bathing then, and did our best with "what we'd got". We had never heard of showers, except in the context of rain showers which filled our water butts and gave us lovely soft water to wash in. In fact, we had to wait for it to rain before we could wash our hair; we never used hard water from the pump, unless absolutely necessary, for fear of spoiling the texture of our hair. We had different values then, you see. We believed that constant washing ruined hair: once every three weeks to a month was quite enough; and we were never allowed to wash our hair or feet during a period – excepting for one of our school mates, Daisy, who had her hair washed every day after school. Our mothers were horrified at this and forecast that she would be bald by the time she was twenty. I don't *think* she was?

As well as having fantastically healthy hair (through lack of washing), I think we were healthier generally during the war: although some expert or other will be sure to tell us that we weren't. Our food being well-controlled, we didn't over-eat, as we do now; and most people didn't have the time to become hypochondriacs.

There were exceptions, of course: many sailors suffered from tuberculosis after years spent abroad in a hot climate, and usually they died. T.B. was the main dread of most people then – I can't remember anyone in our vicinity collapsing and dying suddenly from a heart attack. We also had frequent colds and bouts of bronchitis, and poor old Mr "Big" Sam Smith suffered continually with hay-fever. We used to hear him sneezing and coughing away in his garden and how we giggled and made fun. Why? – he was a nice, harmless old man. (Incidentally, we had Big Sam living down the road, Little Sam living up the road, and a third Mr Sam Smith – our sexton at the church!) Why do we laugh at such things as hay fever, bunions, floating kidneys and water on the brain? I suppose it's a form of nervous embarrassment. Mother was telling us one day about a local man who had had a plate put in his head during the 1914 War, and suddenly started to laugh. Joining in, we screamed and shrieked. Being very young at the time, I imagined she meant an enamel dinner plate, similar to the one that Dad had his dinner from when it had to be kept warm in the oven. I'm sure that I stared at this poor man for years, trying to see the rim of the plate protruding from the back of his head.

On went the war. Dad continued to riddle slack from the coal, our only form of heating (allowance – five cwt per month), and grumble about the Germans. I remember one dance at the local pub, which was held to raise money to buy a spitfire. I think we managed to raise about ten pounds in all. A Spitfire cost a little more than that, I think. The landlord sang 'Just A Song At Twilight', his son sang 'Friend O' Mine', a searchlight soldier, George Pavey, sang 'Only A Rose', while I flirted with the drummer in the band, who kept trying to hold my hand in the dark: quite exciting, I felt, but he was a little bit frightening!

CHAPTER 12

PUBS AND MUSIC

Music played a large part in our wartime lives. Apart from Bing Crosby and Charlie Kunz on our beloved wireless – which was treated like another member of the family; we had wonderful get-together sing-songs; the pub songs were great, such as had never been heard before, or since.

Some of our adopted soldier friends had good voices and varied repertoires. The local searchlight soldiers were mostly Welsh, so there were plenty of outstanding voices from that quarter. If we were lucky enough to have a pianist in the company, it was great, but if we didn't, the Welsh contingency carried on regardless, finishing up the evening with 'Land Of My Fathers', for which, out of courtesy to them, we all stood to attention; and 'God Save The King', for which we also stood to attention, singing loud and heartily – and meaning it too!

One night a stranger sitting in the bar, didn't rise for the accustomed national anthem; when prodded and poked, he sneered cynically and said he didn't believe in such things. The landlady, a dramatic ex-stage star, nearly had hysterics. She said to her husband: "Harry! Harry! Do something!"

Harry, a *very* large man, strode across the room and hauled the little man by the collar to his feet. Holding him thus, we all bawled out: "God Save the King!"

Afterwards, the landlady, eyes flashing, shouted: "We're all

British here, I hope." We cheered and clapped, while the little rebel slunk out of the door, with landlord Harry's words ringing in his ears: "And don't ever bother to come back!" Such were the sentiments of the time.

One soldier had a deep bass voice and could sometimes be persuaded to sing 'Texas Dan', which had the deepest notes possible. That was a great favourite. Then soldier George Pavey would sing: he had a beautifully trained tenor voice and could sometimes be heard singing while on guard at the gun-site by the river. It was lovely to hear 'The Wedding Of The Painted Doll' floating over the water on a moonlit night, as we crossed the bridge. Soldier Eddie Nightingale (belying his name), however, couldn't sing a note.

A local lad Ray Perkins sang "I'll take you home again, Kathleen, to where your father's never been", and Irene and I sang in harmony "Ramona". "I dread the dawn when I awake and find you gorn," we blared out, amid much giggling. Dad occasionally sang too; 'A Farmer's Boy' was his party piece. He hadn't a good voice: he sang too much down his nose; and when he got up to sing his other party piece, which Mother considered a rude song ('It's As Far As I Want To Go'), we all arose in disgust and either disappeared into our handkerchiefs or the "Ladies" – whichever was the most convenient at the time. It was a very mild rude song really, but we didn't like to see our staid parents making fools of themselves.

Dad had always possessed a melodian (a sort of small accordian), and used to play it for celebrations and such like. The last occasion was V.E. (Victory in Europe) night, when he played it so long and hard that it broke completely in half!

Many unusual songs appeared during the war that now seem completely forgotten, sadly:

Some chicken, some neck,
Some chicken, by heck!

– conceived from the Churchill speech. There was also:

Hey! little hen, when, when, when,
Will you lay me an egg for my tea?
Hey! little hen, when, when, when,
Will you try to supply one for me?
Get upon your nest, do your little best,
Get it off your chest, I can do the rest,
Hey! little hen, when, when,when,
Will you lay me an egg for my tea?

and –

My sister and I remember still,
A Tulip garden by an old Dutch mill,
And a home that was all our own until –
But we don't talk about that.

My sister and I recall once more,
The fishing steamer pulling from the shore,
And the dog cart we drove in days before –
But we don't talk about that.

We're trying to forget the fear,
That came from the troubled sky,
We're almost happy over here,
But sometimes we wake at night and cry –

My sister and I recall the day,
We said 'goodbye' and then we sailed away,
But we think of those friends that had to stay –
But we don't talk about that.

This song was written by a Dutch refugee or rather by a brother and sister.

I remember another song written by a young aircraftman named Collins who longed to fly. One day his obsession overcame him and he took off into the blue, flying the plane he was supposed to be fitting! (something like that anyway). We sympathised with him, and were delighted to read in the paper that he eventually *did* gain his wings.

If I only had wings,
Oh! what a difference it would make to things.
All day long I'd be in the sky,
Up on high,
Talking to the birdies that passed me by.
How the fellows would stare,
To see me roaring past them through the air,
Never tiring of the thrill it brings.
If I only had wings.

I'd be so fearless and bold,
That when the stories of my deeds were told,
You'd see my picture in the paper,
And you would hear them say,
The R.A.F. and me just had another good day.

If I only had wings.
One little pair of those elusive things,
You would never hear me complain again.
If I only had wings,
If I only had wings.

Of course, there were also the well-known and much remembered songs –

White cliffs of Dover,
Yours,
Amapola.

My particular favourites were as follows –

What a surprise for the Duce, the Duce,
He can't put it over the Greeks,
Oh! what a surprise for the Duce. They do say,
He's had no spaghetti for weeks,
His Troubadours advance with roars,
of 'Viva el Viva!'
With armoured cars they strum guitars,
While, frilly white skirts, play the 'deuce' with black shirts,
Oh! what a surprise for the Duce, for the Duce,
He can't put it over the Greeks!

The Duce was Mussolini, the Italian leader and our enemy, who was hob-nobbing with Hitler when this song came out. Mussolini was fighting the Greeks, who were reputed to go into battle wearing their ceremonial white skirts. True or false? I can't say!

Norman Long, a comedian classed as "all teeth and trousers", sang:

Mr Schmidt with his Messerschmitt,
Up in the bright blue sky.
Schmidt loved Messerschmitts,

There's no doubt,
Always took one with him,
Couldn't fly without
(Line missing)
Couldn't land without a parachute,
But one day the silly clown,
Went and landed upside down,
And the Messerschmitt,
Made a proper mess-a-schmitt!"

and –

Mr Brown of London town, had a job to do,
Meant to see it through, and he did it too.
Mr Brown of London town, sent the wife away,
Sent his kids to play, miles and miles away.
Things blew up, things blew down, seemed a blinkin' shame.
Lots of fire and flame, Blimey! what a game!
But who stood up and saved the town,
When London bridge was falling down,
Mr Brown of London town. Hi! Mr Brown.

A song very popular with girls who were courting R.A.F. men (or thinking about it) was –

Some people say that he is just a crazy guy,
To me he means a million other things.
An ordinary fella in a uniform of blue,
He wears a pair of silver wings.

Sometimes when I'm alone and he is far away,
I sometimes wonder what tomorrow brings,
For I adore that crazy guy, who taught my heart to fly,
He wears a pair of silver wings.

The girls – who were courting the R.A.F. men – went very coy and proud when this song was sung. Needless to say, almost all their fellas were ground staff and that didn't carry anything like the prestige of an actual flyer.

To "land" a pilot, or someone wearing wings on his breast, was the ultimate accolade. I only knew of one local lad who got his wings – there must have been others. His name was John and he was so handsome, he looked too good to be true. He had a lovely voice as well and most girls *must* have had a crush on him. I know I did. He was a bit of a "one-off" though, and he was very stand-offish with the village girls. The lads weren't very keen on him – jealous, I suppose. They tried to pretend to us that they thought he was a bit cranky, because he had once lived in Canada. Well, that was a bit strange, I suppose! He also, in his less aloof moments, could do a good impression of Hitler!

Around this time, Gracie Fields, our greatest singing favourite, champion of charity work, and all-round entertainer, fell from grace (if you'll pardon the pun): with her marriage to Italian, Monty Banks. We sort of banished her from our lives. It was all very unfortunate. She had been so popular and so good-hearted, but I don't think she ever regained her status in this country. And there was still Vera Lynn and Anne Shelton, whom we very much admired. Our friend Edna at the lock house had a piano which she played (not very well). We insisted on buying her pieces of popular music, sixpence a time, to entertain us with in patriotic fashion. We used to go round to her house every night to sing. How her poor mother must have suffered! We foraged through her music stool, searching for antiquated pieces that we could get our teeth into, like 'Rule Brittania', but usually we ended up with 'Apple Blossom Time', 'You'd Be So Nice To Come Home To', and 'Jim', which we sang nevertheless, with gusto.

Edna was courting a young fellow named Jim at the time, so she'd sing:

> *Jim never seems to buy me pretty flowers,*
> *Jim, never comes to cheer my lonely hours.*
> *Don't know why I'm so crazy for Jim,*
> *Jim never tells me I'm his hearts desire.*
> *I never seem to set his heart on fire,*
> *Don't know why I'm so crazy for him, and so on!*

Another song of the time was 'Hey Mabel'. Mother, whose name was Mabel, had a running joke with the searchlight soldiers, that when the searchlight flashed across the sky at night, they would be sending out a signal to her: "Hey! Mabel, wait for me!" Great laughs were had in the Local over this.

It may seem that we spent a lot of our young lives in the local pub; well, in a way I suppose we did. In a small community such as ours the wartime pubs developed into social centres; there, we could meet friends and acquaintances, keep up with the local news, have a laugh and a joke, a bit of music, relax and let the tensions of the war float away. Remember, we had no television then, and with such an influx of different people, particularly servicemen, the place became a focal point of interest to a lot of people.

Lots of women, my mother included, had never set foot in a public bar before the war. It wasn't a matter of just going to drink: my mother, sister and I and our girl friends could exist on a shandy each for a couple of hours – and still have a rip-roaring good time;

sometimes we could sit with friends without bothering to have a drink at all!

It would be of interest to note that whenever an American bought us a drink, a shandy or sometimes beer, it would always be by the pint; so much liquid to consume, filled us girls with great amusement and sense of confusion! We never had too much to drink: the nearest we came to being "merry" was on one glass of cider. Some of the men got a bit squiffy but I can honestly say that acts of disorderly conduct were few and far between.

As we walked the mile home from the bus stop after going to the pictures in town, we would often call in one pub or another, just to see what was going on and who was new. The pub's atmosphere of the Twenties and Thirties, the "all man's province" was gradually phased out – though the pubs of the Eighties: food, chicken in a basket and electric fittings, had yet to come into being.

Those were the Olympian days, and the swan song of the real public house.

CHAPTER 13

CLOTHES MAKETH THE MAN
AND WOMEN MAKETH THE CLOTHES!

The day before clothes rationing was declared operational, Mother took me to Worcester and bought me a dress, two petticoats and a vest with a fancy top, so I was considered very lucky. The dress, which was a very cheap flowered cotton, cost three shillings & eleven pence (20p), and the vest, of which I was very proud, having up to then worn only round-necked vests in children's and men's style, cost one shilling & eleven pence (10p). I can't recall the price of the petticoats.

All through childhood, we had had clothes passed on to us from our auntie, which were of excellent quality. When the war plunged us into the cheap utility-style material, there was a vast difference and even I, in my youthful ignorance, could see it. Shoes squeaked, coat linings rustled like paper and there was no smoothness in the cloth. Even the wool we bought seemed harder.

As the war continued, we made do with all sorts of things, including having to undo and re-knit old jumpers. By post, we could buy surplus sub-standard parachutes for five shillings (25p) and no coupons. They were made of silk and usually white, sometimes a brilliant yellow. Later on, nylon parachutes came on the market. We undid the seams and made knickers, petticoats and nightdresses with them. This was alright if you were a dab hand with a needle, but I was a hopeless sewer and quickly got so bored with unpicking seams, that I ended up with very odd underwear: large thick seams going down the middle and in all directions. I couldn't have worn them for best but they did for every-day use – as long as I didn't get knocked over, that is! Mother made my sister a nightdress out of one of these parachutes. It was huge and flowing: we called it "the bloater skin"

My sister, who was then in her late teens, took to wearing hats on most occasions – trilbys usually. I have a photograph of her lolling up against a gate, wearing a trilby and glasses: she looked a cross between Carroll Gibbons and Al Capone.

We knitted and knitted as much as we could. I found a pattern for a pixie-hood in a wool shop. I knitted it and wore it to school – it was just the thing to keep the ears warm when riding my bicycle.

Popular knitting patterns of the time

I received very funny looks at the time from the young, new infant teacher who had never seen one before, but it wasn't long before everyone was wearing knitted hoods. They were a huge fashion, being practical and warm and could be made out of oddments of wool. I knitted one for Auntie Bo and she really took to it – she continued to wear hoods until she died.

I knitted one jumper, in pink three-ply wool, which took eight ounces and cost threepence an ounce. You couldn't get much more of a bargain! We pounced on all bargains, then. A Mrs Bullock from Wolverhampton, who was one of our left-over customers from the fruit and flower days, used to bring me a lot of clothes which her daughter had outgrown. One of these garments, a plain brown cardigan, I unpicked and knitted into a jumper with a ribbed yolk, on which I embroidered some funny looking flowers in bright colours. Unfortunately, the jumper had short sleeves and made my arms look too thin – Mother said I would catch cold in short sleeves, so that was a wasted economy.

Mrs Bullock also brought me a white coat, which I hated on sight, as it had old-fashioned lapels. But then I went to see Dorothy Lamour in *The Fleet's In* at Droitwich Salters Hall cinema. She was wearing a white tie-belted coat like mine (well – a *bit* like), so I felt more kindly disposed towards it after that and wore it all the time. It made me look exactly like Dorothy Lamour, of course! I even tried doing my hair the same way. At this time we wore turbans on our hair – another Dorothy Lamour fashion – smart ones for going out and less smart to work in. Some of us had our hair drifting languidly over one side of the face like Veronica Lake, others parted their hair in the middle, similar to Hedy Lamarr, who was very glamourous. Then along came Betty Grable and up went our hair in bunches of top curls, Edwardian style. During this period we lived seventy-five percent of our lives in dinky curlers and wore snoods on our hair; this was probably a fashion started in armament factories to keep girls' hair from catching in the machinery. Mother called them "snooges" and Dad called them "sprout nets".

The idea with the new clothing coupons was that if you bought clothes from mail order or by post, you cut out the coupons from your book; clothing shops would not accept loose coupons, so if you had managed to get hold of some loose ones, that is how you shopped. There was a lot of black-marketeering going on with clothing coupons, as with food.

When we got friendly with a couple of travelling girls, Phyllis and Rosie who worked on the land and were not too interested in new clothes, we used to trade our second-hands for their coupons; everyone was happy. This of course was illegal, but lots of deals went on in the war. We didn't consider we were doing anything outrageous in the climate of the times. We were quite happy to get hold of a few illegal coupons or a little bit of "under the counter" food – not too much though! For the law-abiding honest people of Britain that we were then, it was nice to feel a bit naughty.

During a holiday at Bournemouth, I saw a lovely coat for sale in one of the "posher" shops and fell for it in a big way. It was scarlet with an attached cape: a very spectacular coat, but I hadn't enough coupons in my book! I had a few loose ones, however, and reached an agreement with the sales lady: I passed over my coupons from the book and hurried round to the Post Office, whereupon I mailed the loose ones by express delivery. After about an hour, I could go and collect the coat. Unfortunately, it was too long and I had to spend the afternoon in Bournemouth sea-front gardens, pinning and stitching up the hem! But I couldn't wait to wear it. After the years of austerity, it looked so glamourous. Incidentally, on the day I sat sewing up my coat in the town of Bournemouth, Neville George Heath, a notorious murderer of the day, was in the nearby chines committing another murder of a young girl. He was eventually hanged.

Some of the clothing tricks we got up to were quite amazing. We used to put patches on patches on patches – I can even remember putting a large patch on my lisle stockings! Then I heard that if I bought enough of the thread we used to mend the stockings, I could actually knit my own – with perseverance. I did about six inches before my patience (like Hitler's) became exhausted. It was too tedious for words. The little cards of thread were a penny and twopence and we had plenty left to mend our stockings with for years – thanks to my negative efforts.

Another time, Auntie Nellie sent us masses of stockings with great holes under the feet. Rose's mother used to walk about with no shoes on, "holeing" her stockings as she went, before eventually abandoning them for bare legs. Auntie said: "They will be useful for you, the legs are good!" We wore them – imagine! It doesn't seem credible but the holes in silk and rayon didn't run into ladders as they do now.

I also started to read the *Lady* magazines which were passed on to me. I found great bargains to be had in second-hand clothes here. I sent away to one lady in Tunbridge Wells, for a pair of brown and white calf-skin shoes with perforated fronts, price fifteen shillings (75p). They were size five and a half which was too big for me, but they were also narrow and the toes pinched. So I never wore them and they didn't fit anyone else in the household. What a silly thing to do! I laid them to rest underneath the washstand upstairs and here they remained throughout the war and long after, gathering dust. I wonder what happened to them.

The sale of some second-hand clothes then was a dirty business and us buyers were terribly exploited. We got so feverish to have new things, it was like an addiction. Dad started mending our shoes. He bought pairs of round rubbers and would hammer them on to the heels of poor old Mum's shoes. She hated them because they looked so odd. Dad never trimmed them to fit the shape of the heel, so she lurched along in a peculiar fashion, with Dad peering suspiciously and inspecting them nightly to ensure that she was turning the rubber around, as instructed, to avoid wear.

At one point I had a pair of Lancashire wooden clogs; they were ugly and clumsy but I loved them and I pitched and hobbled along on them through the war years like a martyr. They could be bought without coupons and were a present from my aunt, who had a friend in Bolton – Nannie Mattie of the horse manure fame.

When wooden-soled shoes came into being, we all wore them. They were smart and took less coupons, on account of the wood. I was able to buy a second-hand pair in new condition for four shillings, sixpence (22½p). I also had sixpence knocked off for the squeak, which disappeared anyway after I poured liquid parafin into the hinge. These hinged soles were much better than my proper clogs which had no "give" in the sole at all.

So we staggered through the war, with our "seconds" and patches and our "make do and mends". Classes of "make do and mend" started in the village hall and the women's magazines were amass with wonderful hints for putting new collars on dresses, tarting up plain garments with bits of floral material, and adding length with false hems.

At the beginning of the war, Mother joined a knitting and sewing party, run by Mrs Pepy's-Cockerel who lived at the castle. Mum and her chums walked up every Wednesday afternoon for meetings and tea. Their output was terrific. We girls helped to knit some of the garments, like balaclava helmets and socks. The wool with which we used to knit sea-boot stockings for the navy was thick, oily and smelly, but it made our hands beautifully soft. One day, priority instructions came for the ladies to knit officers' cardigans for use in very cold climates. They were to be very special, and the knitters worked hard and long into the early hours to get them completed; only to find later that some had been given to the officers at the local searchlight posts, who were, to put it mildly, living the life of Riley! The ladies were a bit narked at that.

The group eventually became members of the W.V.S. and were awarded badges. The garments completed during the war by the nineteen members amounted to 1,172. My mother's output was sixty-five garments, which included socks, gloves, mittens, gum-boot stockings, sea-boot stockings, balaclava helmets, scarves, cardigans, operating socks and stockings, and children's vests. They were sent to H.M. Forces, Mercantile Marine, British P.O.Ws, Russian Forces, Yugoslavian P.O.Ws, Military and Civilian Hospitals.

CHAPTER 14

THE POWER OF THE PEN

As we had no telephones or other means of communication, we had always written a lot of letters to relatives, near and far, and to one another. Telegrams were sent only as emergencies and most people were reduced to nothing less than frozen terror at the sight of them.

My mother's family were all enthusiastic writers. The uncles sent many letters detailing their exploits in the Boer War and the Great War, while our aunts kept post-card albums and wrote copiously from all parts of the British Isles between 1900 and 1920. I still have many of these letters and all the post cards, which mostly have trivial little messages:

Dearest Flo,

Hope your cold is better,

love from your devoted sister, Nell.

Dearest Mother,

I have tried on the corsets and think they will fit you,

Fondest love, Florrie.

P.S. Hope dear Dad is well, give him my fondest love.

When Mother was rushed into hospital with a perforated appendix, we children went to stay with Auntie Bo. It was January and we picked masses of snowdrops from the back orchard to send to hospital with notes which said:

Dear Mammy,
Hope you will soon be better,
love from J.

and –

Dear Mammy,
Hope you will soon be better,
love from M.

We always called her Mammy as children, I think it was a hangover from the Al Jolson period.

When I was about twelve, I had a pen-friend, Mary Duncan from Scotstown, Glasgow. We wrote similarly formed letters: "Hope you are well. Write soon. Love J.", and ditto to me from Mary!

During the war, we wrote and wrote and wrote. We wrote to stray soldiers we met on buses, at dances or in the pubs. We wrote to American soldiers, via their mates at Westwood Park. I had an American pen-friend named Henry Lee. There was a popular song of the time –

Hey, round the corner, hoo, hoo
Behind the berry tree.
Hey round the footpath, behind the bush,
Looking for Henry Lee!

– so that was exciting for me. We were friendly with a searchlight soldier named Percy, a little tiny chap about five feet tall. I wrote to his brother Noel who was in the Burma jungle, hoping that he was taller than his brother Percy, in case I ever met him.

Our searchlight was situated at the top of the hill by the school in the village, where it could pick up any aircraft passing through at night, especially towards Birmingham. We also had a gun of some description standing by the river to catch any Germans coming up it. When the soldiers stationed at these locations left us and went on to different postings, we wrote to them. We wrote to our friend Irene's three brothers who were all in the army and when I say we, I mean *all* the girls in our gang. We wrote to a neighbour, Doug Smith, who was a petty officer on *H.M.S. Warspite;* we sent him birthday and Christmas cards, hoping that he would get them in time – I think he usually did! which was amazing to say the least!

I wrote regularly to Tom who was a sailor on *H.M.S. Wedgeport.* I wrote to him for about a year and received approximately three letters every week from him, telling me how he had been "dhobiing" the decks and what the weather was like.

Boy, did we write! We wrote hundreds of letters; it was a status symbol with us girls to see how many fellows we could correspond with – and it counted more if they were abroad. It was the same way that we competed to see how many different fellows we could get to walk us home – and they had to be in uniform, otherwise it didn't count – no notches on the gun that night. I met one soldier named Wally, while having an illicit drink in the Red Lion. He was exceptionally nice, and distinctive in that he had a streak of white through his hair. He was probably about thirty and had not long been back from Dunkirk. I only met him twice for a drink and a walk home. He went away with my address and I forgot about him; weeks later I was surprised to receive a very emotional letter, telling me that he was madly in love with me, and could he come and see me on leave, as I was the only girl he had ever loved, signed Walter. I didn't answer, it seemed so silly. He had probably seen me for about two hours and I was only about fifteen years old!

The war did strange things to the letter writing community; I suppose it was on account of the chaps being away from all that was dear to them in their lives, their families and homes.

My friend Irene and I were horrified and then amused to receive an identical letter from one Albert, a sailor vowing his undying love for us both! This was a bit daft on his part, as Irene and I were working together at the time and he should have known that we would compare letters.

One night, while having a drink in the Local with Mother, we got talking to a chap wearing civvies (civilian clothes); he was a tall, weedy-looking youth with terrible acne and he told us a frightful tale of how his whole family had been killed in an air-raid and he himself had been gravely wounded at Dunkirk. Warming to his subject he said, his voice choking with emotion, that his one ambition was to get back into the army and give his all for his country to revenge the terrible deaths of his family.

Well – I can tell you he had us spellbound with pity, the tears welling in our eyes, until a few days later, P.C. Shaylor exploded his story with a sarcastic: "What! that Jimmy G. . ., he's never been away from the village in his life, and his parents are living in the new council houses on the green, alive and well!" (The village was a few miles from ours, so, I suppose, not unlike a foreign land.) To add insult to injury, when he really was called up into the army, this Jimmy G. . . wrote to my mother, putting on the letter his name, number and "February 2nd Squad"! "February 2nd" became his nickname after this.

When he turned up on leave, he was completely oblivious, full of pep, and uncaring about the lies he had told us. What is more, he walked into the bar of the Local, stood up by the piano and sang 'The Boys of Old Flanigan's Band', to the tune of 'MacNamara's Band' – and had the audacity to tell us he had written it! Ugh! we detested him after that and put him down as a crank.

Most soldiers, sailors and airmen wrote on the back of their envelopes such things as, "S.W.A.L.K." – which meant "Sealed with a loving kiss"; "H.O.L.L.A.N.D." – "Hope our love lasts and never dies"; and "I.T.A.L.Y." – "I trust and love you". This was a custom which *I* hated, as it usually didn't mean anything to them or us. We were not in love with them and if we were, we didn't trust them and certainly never wanted our loves to last and never die! Anyway, we always had our eyes *wide* open for anyone more promising to come along, like American millionaires or landed gentry.

CHAPTER 15

THE HOUSE

In my youth it wasn't fashionable to live in a cottage. The envied children lived in red-brick, semi-detached, square houses, with large windows – circa 1900-1930-type. Our cottage, which we rented at first, was very attractive, painted cream and brown, with Dutch gabling and diamond-paned windows. When we moved in, in the early Thirties, the cottage was decorated throughout. It had been empty for years. The landlord, Mr Partridge, had originally bought it for he and his wife to live in, for £200. Mr Partridge, being of a delicate nature, then decided that living near the river – a field away – would not be beneficial to his health, so it remained empty.

A builder named Jauncey went to work on it, papering, painting and removing and smashing most of the blue Delft tiles surrounding the grate. My mother salvaged about a dozen of these tiles (six of which I still have) to use as plant pot stands and tea pot stands.

The cottage was very pretty, like a dolls house, and much admired and photographed by passers-by. It was not so convenient to live in, however, excepting that it was detached, with a large garden surrounding. Dad found he couldn't quarrel with the near neighbours so easily, although he did his best!

The garden was large and quite interesting, with an old cherry tree, which Dad soon felled and a pear tree, which he did likewise.

The snowdrops and other dainty little spring flowers, we kept. Dad soon cleared and created a beautiful garden, although *we* secretly mourned the old trees.

Buried in the garden was the skeleton of a horse, and our little unattached shed was its old stable, a large hole being worn down in the middle of the brick floor from the horse's feet. The bones of the horse were re-buried several times in later years, when first one water pipe, then another and then the sewerage system were laid. When Dad first discovered the bones, Mother and us children were very upset: Mother thinking of the hard times it must have had in the past, us children crying bitterly in support. We learned that the horse used to pull a trap for its previous owners, the Benbows, whose son lived at the Wharf Hotel, and had had the house built for them.

At the centre of the front of the cottage was a little porch made of brick, with a gabled roof, lovely coloured tiles on the floor, a wooden seat which was always a mass of milk bottles, sticks, keys, dog-leads, collars, messages etc to tradesmen; and two little slit openings to look through. As I grew up, these proved invaluable to me when wishing to keep a sharp lookout for fellas that I either did or did not fancy. On seeing a fancied one coming down the road, I could sidle out, simperingly and pretend to be surprised to see him; a non-fancied one, on the other hand, would send me hastily inside to hide. The slits were also useful for leaping out of to wave to butcher, baker or paper-boys, who were also down for a fancy.

On the walls we wrote the registration numbers of cars belonging to the locals. There weren't many then, of course. OJ 6497 was the number of Police Sergeant Stockton's Austin 7. Sergeant Stockton was a very stern policeman, but fair. We liked him because, with his loud voice, he could really put the rowdy campers in their place.

From the porch we went straight into the sitting-room, which for some strange reason we called the "house"! In here, half kitchen, half sitting room, stood a black cast-iron grate, the centre of both the room and our existence – then. The fire was always kept lit, except during a heat wave, and even then Dad prowled moodily about, mourning for it: a warm fireside and enough food to eat had been a great luxury to country people when he was a boy, so I think he saw it as some sort of symbol.

The hobs were always laden with kettles boiling or saucepans simmering, and a draw plate was balanced on the top. In winter, the hobs usually held a jar of homemade wine, which Dad drank hot to ward away colds and chills. There would also be a large stone hot-water bottle warming. When the stone bottles got broken, Dad used a big cider jar instead, as it was impossible to renew *anything* in wartime.

On one side of the fire was the oven. This oven was a marvel; in it Mother cooked the meat, the roast, the baked potatoes, all the puddings and lovely cakes. During winter we also used it to store firewood (which occasionally started to smoulder and had to be rushed outside), our smaller hot-water bottles, Dad's slippers and socks, and the aforesaid comics; and on ironing days, the door was left ajar, draped over with small clean clothes for airing.

One of Mother's greatest enthusiasms was airing. She aired everything, including tablecloths, tea towels and handkerchiefs (both sides); she would then press them to her face and glow with pleasure at their warm smell. The rest of the ironing would be draped over chairs in front of the fire; the chairs being polished wood, dining-room style, would sometimes become so hot that the varnish would bubble and blister. Mother didn't mind – as long as we were all safe from the perils of damp clothes.

In the ceiling of the "house" were four large hooks, which had been used to hang bacons and dried foods in the old days. We used them to hang washing lines from in wet spells. From childhood, I disliked this intensely – it all seemed so poverty-like to me.

Nothing was nicer than for all the washing to be cleared away and actually being able to see the warm bright fire.

Also in the centre of the room stood the large wooden table on which we had our meals, peeled vegetables, chopped things up, made cakes, did the famous ironing – with the flat irons heated on the trivet by the fire – washed up sometimes, cleaned boots and shoes, and washed children.

Over the table was a large hanging lamp. Every other day in winter, this would be filled with parafin and the glass polished by huffing and puffing into it and rubbing it up with a duster (being *terribly* careful not to crack the glass in doing so).

This lamp was another worry to Mother who, fearing the parafin might have leaked out, spent a lot of time sniffing at food. Mother always sniffed her food before eating (as I believe General Montgomery also did) for fear of poison. She would have been a great asset in the Borgias' reign.

The "house" was overcrowded with furnishings as Mother used to buy so many bargains at sales and would cram them in haphazardly. A spice cupboard, a Victorian whatnot, a large table, a small table, the sideboard, a sofa, two armchairs, four other chairs, a milking stool, a bookcase and large pictures all over the walls, completed the "house", which measured approximately twelve square feet. The floor was just bricks and earth, no damp course or concrete then. We mainly had oil-cloth and coconut matting as covering, but we did have a large cotton rug for the hearth, which we put down on Sundays, high days and if visitors were expected.

We bought our rugs and mats off the oil man and paid about one shilling (5p) a week towards the cost, having a little card with the amount entered. Though we didn't consider this "hire purchase", we never mentioned it to Dad, who would not have approved: "Don't tell your father that I'm paying for this weekly," Mother, who never put the mats down until she had paid up the money on the card, would say.

The "house" led into the middle room, so called because no one could decide what its purpose was. It was really too small for anything. We did go through spasms of calling it the kitchen, but we never *kitched* in it, if you see what I mean. It mostly stored things that we didn't know what to do with, and Dad's geraniums in winter; the bogey-hole under the stairs was also in there, full of junk, old shoes, pictures and mice. Next door was the pantry, larger than average, as big as the middle room in fact, and very nice and cold.

The last room downstairs was the scullery, which housed the copper for washing, a brown crock sink and a big cast iron range with "Bonnybridge Dover" engraved on it. In summer time, Mother cooked the joint in this, but she wasn't keen on it. Round the walls were brick shelves, on which stood interesting bottles and tins, and rat, mole and gin traps. One particularly interesting bottle, green with a red and white label, was marked "Poison". We children couldn't reach these shelves.

The scullery was the place where Dad took his chums at homemade wine time, and Mr Davies on bath nights! It was also where we kept our bicycles, Freddie and Bartholomew. (Dad kept his post-office cycle in the shed, having fitted a padlock to the door, and thereby convincing the post-office authorities of its absolute safety in all circumstances. The post-office was a very rigid society at that time.)

Up from the "house" led the narrow and twisted staircase. The largest upstairs room had once, in its history, been enlarged; it had no door and I think had been a landing bedroom. It was a very funny shape and had a sloping ceiling. The parent's brass bedstead, being the largest item in the crowded room, only just fitted in. A pine chest of drawers, that Mother had painted and varnished over and over, contained a paraphanalia of little treasures: brushes and combs;

powder and starch; cream and ointments; a large bottle of *Harlene* hair tonic, which had the tiniest screw top imaginable and from which I pinched drops occasionally to make my hair more beautiful; *California Poppy* perfume; hair pins; nets; slides; mirrors; photographs; peppermints and toffees, in and out of wrappers; the list was endless – whether that chest was ever dusted off I'm not sure! As I grew older, I attempted to tidy Mother up. She was grateful, but couldn't understand the necessity.

The little bedroom for us girls was a square-shaped room, with another cast iron fire-place with brown wood surround, in which a fire was lit when we were ill. The ceiling was covered in large interesting cracks and, lying in our beds, we used to imagine all sorts of stories, the shapes and contours of the cracks seeming like mountains, clouds and seas.

We had a bed each and feather mattresses. My sister's iron-framed bed was bought at Powers Farm sale and was always referred to as Bertha Wakem, after its former occupant. My bed was more modern, wooden with a very weak frame which wriggled and squeaked.

Other items in the room included the wicker chair, which also squeaked, a wooden table with a swivel mirror, and a wooden wash-stand with a lovely pink china basin and a white jug with pink roses on; it also had a large crack down the side. We kept rainwater upstairs for washing, which of course had to be emptied downstairs via the slop bucket. When it was a really cold winter, the water froze in the jug.

Under the beds were boxes and suitcases, full of clothes and books and a chamber pot for each of us. We also stored apples there and were grateful one winter, when all confined to bed with 'flu, for this instant food.

Candles, which we carried up and downstairs, were used to light both bedrooms. On our bedroom walls was another conglomeration of pictures bought at sales; calendars and our beloved pin-ups. My sister had Alan Jones, Stewart Grainger and various war heros such as Wing Commander Paddy Finugane, who was later shot down in his plane. I had Raymond Massey, Kings Farouk, Zog and George V, and a cut-out of Ronald Coleman standing proudly by the side of a giant sword-fish he had caught, which towered above him.

The windows in both bedrooms were diamond-paned, iron-framed and very high and safe for children. In the eaves of the roof, starlings and sparrows twittered, quarrelled and fought late into the night and the occasional rat could be heard scurrying around. Once, a bat came flying in and was chased wildly round the bedroom by Dad in his night-shirt, while we children huddled terrified under the bed-clothes.

In the garden was a cast-iron pump of the real, old cottage variety. We relied largely on the rain water which "droppeth from the sky above". In winter when the pump froze, it had to be primed by pouring a kettle of boiling water down through the works. In summer it often dried up. But all in all, it was pretty reliable, unlike many country pumps.

On the lawn at the corner of the cottage was an ancient yew tree, and underneath, a homemade wooden bench-type seat. There was also a wooden-framed canvas stall for the selling of vegetables and fruit and anything else going – until one Sunday afternoon when a motor-bike shot through the hedge and demolished it; after that we just sold at the gate.

We had no dust-bins and no refuse collection; rubbish was either burned or buried, which didn't involve much work, as we had hardly any tinned food. When we went to live in the cottage, the garden contained a proper rubbish tip which I wish was available to me now, when I think of the old bottles that must have been buried.

The dear little lavatory was like a mini house in itself. It had a long wooden seat, with one hole for adults and one for children. The adult side had a wooden lid with a shaped handle, and the children's had a cruder version with a large nail to lift it. The buckets underneath had to be emptied into a hole in the garden. We had newspaper for the wiping of bottoms; we cut up paper into squares and pierced the corners with scissors; the pieces would then be hung up by string on a nail on the wall.

It was a popular pastime in the winter, when we hadn't much to occupy us, cutting up paper for the lavatory; the *Radio Times* was our favourite, the paper being particularly soft then, and the shape just right! Also in the lavatory, we hung things of interest: yet more mole and rat traps, hooks, scythes and garden shears and more pin-ups – not very flattering to our heroes! Many of our pretty calendars finished up on the walls, along with interesting articles in newspapers. The Abdication, the Jubilee, the Coronation, Royal weddings, births of Royal babies, all ended up on our lavatory wall for us to sit and peruse in comfort. During the war, Churchill and the Cabinet, Hitler, Mussolini and their cronies also joined this illustrious picture gallery.

I think we must have enjoyed going to visit the lavatory – apart from the smell, which could be pretty atrocious at times; of course, other peoples lavatories smelt *much* worse than ours. It was peaceful and we could read to our hearts' content – except in winter, when the seat sparkled with ice and the candle flame threatened to flicker out in the cold air.

For the cottage, garden and all concerned, we paid six shillings and sixpence a week rent (33p); Dad said this was "daylight robbery" for such an old draughty inconvenient shack, and that *they* ought to be shot for having the cheek to charge such a price.

THE END

I do not recall at what point we country dwellers realised that the war was coming to an end. Dad and his First World War chums were of the opinion that we should carry on until no Germans were left living to start yet another one, which, if he (Dad) had had his way we should have done in 1918.

"You can't do that," said Mother. "What about Kurt and Sammy Gerson?" – Kurt was a German prisoner whom we had befriended, and Sammy Gerson was a German Jewish searchlight soldier.

"Oh, well, they're alright, I suppose," said Dad uncomfortably. "But you can't trust any of the others."

Mr Churchill told us on the wireless about the fast approaching "V" day – Victory day. Dad made a large wooden "V" and hung it across the road, suspended from two telegraph poles – much to the astonishment of some locals who had probably never heard of "V" day or even of Mr Churchill, for that matter. One day, a tall cattle truck passed by and crashed into the 'V', proceeding on its way with the sign hanging from its roof, ropes dangling

"Would y' *credit* it?" said Dad, "No respect."

Winston Churchill had been a great leader and a tremendous inspiration to us (in spite of what Dad said about him). The King had also been a wartime favourite, so steadfast and unflappable for a reserved man. I remember that lovely speech he made to the nation – "I said to the man who stood at the gate of the year . . . "

Of course, we had had other troubles, apart from the war: my grandfather's death, the death of an uncle – and my sister's attacks of pleurisy. Desperately ill, she had been sent to the tuberculosis sanatorium at Knightwick to recover. This was a harrowing place, encased in sadness and death; although when my sister was feeling better, I think she quite enjoyed the company of the people there and made many friends. In fact, it was probably one of the most peaceful times in her life! Incidentally, it was in the sanatorium she learned to smoke, as most of the patients did!

Visiting her at Knightwick was a difficult business: it was only about six miles away as the crow flies, but as we weren't crows we thought it a very long way to travel to the other side of Worcester. Sometimes, if we were lucky, we got a lift from someone in their car – several locals were in the sanatorium at that time – but mostly the journey entailed two bus rides either way, a mile walk from our house and a great toil up the Ankerdine Hill, carrying bags full of clean clothes and any food that we could manage (the patients were encouraged to eat as much as possible and as many chocolates and sweets as their relatives could muster).

Suddenly, in the Spring of 1945, the morning papers were full of horrifying pictures of Belson. They were the most terrible things we had ever seen. A sort of stunned feeling of mutual mourning reached out to us all, young and old. We couldn't believe that humans could do such dreadful things to their own kind.

"I told you what they were like," said Dad, but even he was stunned.

We had gone periodically to church during the war; at the request of the King we now went to special services to pray for what was left of those poor wretched inmates of the concentration camps.

All our American friends had disappeared into France; we received censored letters from some of them. Then – lo and behold! the end came and everything seemed to go flat.

We lit bonfires and the men got drunk; they burned the handcart belonging to the local publican, who was furious!

"Serves him right," said the men, "he's made enough money out of the war." ("Out of us and our pockets" might have been more correct, but they didn't look at it like that.)

So that was that – the end and the beginning.

There had been only two bombs dropped in our locality, and one plane had crashed by the castle farm, killing the two airmen aboard. Several local servicemen had been killed, wounded or imprisoned; several others had died from tuberculosis. A few marriages had broken up; many babies, illegitimate or in wedlock, had been born.

We had had lots of laughs and topical jokes:

Did you hear about the bull that swallowed a bomb? – It was abominable!

What are the Poles doing in Russia? – Holding up the telegraph wires.

Jerry over – Mop it up in the morning.

Old servilities were dead, women more independent; no more did we curtsey to the lady from the manor or raise our hats to the vicar. We had fought or taken part in a great war, after all; we were *all* as good as the next man, weren't we?

Then came the General Election and the Labour Party got in. I think that many people felt guilty that Churchill had been abandoned. Looking back, it seems strange that after the stalwart way in which he had led the country he was thus passed over. But there it was.

The day the election results were broadcast, I was working at the castle, tidying up the top landing. The assistant matron, Miss Ellis, passed me by, muttering: "A labour government. It's all over, this country is finished" – quite emotionally for her as she was a "tough" nut.

A shiver of fear went through me as she slammed her bedroom door and I was pleased to finish work and get home.

Later, I asked Mother what she thought. She looked worried. "I wonder if they know what to do," she said. "Mr Attlee seems a nice, quiet man, a lot like your grandad."

"Of course they'll be alright," said Dad scornfully. "It should have happened years ago. No more bowing and scraping to the nobs – best thing that ever happened."

"Well, *I* don't know," said Mother.

THE END